A GUIDE TO NATURAL
HOUSEKEEPING

A GUIDE TO NATURAL HOUSEKEEPING

Recipes and solutions for a cleaner, greener home

CHRISTINA STRUTT OF CABBAGES & ROSES

Photography by Lucinda Symons

CICO BOOKS
LONDON NEW YORK

First published in 2008 by CICO Books as *Cabbages & Roses Guide to Natural Housekeeping*
This paperback edition published in 2012 by CICO Books
an imprint of Ryland Peters & Small Ltd
20–21 Jockey's Fields, London WC1R 4BW
www.cicobooks.com

10 9 8 7 6 5 4 3 2 1

A CIP catalogue record for this book is available from the British Library.

Paperback ISBN 978-1-908170-21-7
(Hardback ISBN 978-1-906094-47-8)

Printed in China

Project Editors: Marion Paull, Gillian Haslam
Text Editor: Samantha Gray
Designer: Christine Wood
Photographer: Lucinda Symons
Illustrators: Trina Dalziel, Michael Hill

Always consult a doctor or qualified herbalist before treating any ailment. While every attempt has been made to ensure the information in this book is entirely safe, correct and up-to-date at the time of publication, the Publishers accept no responsibility for consequences of the advice given herein. The Publishers also accept no responsibility for changes in stockists and locations mentioned herein.

CONTENTS

INTRODUCTION

While researching and writing this book, my mood has variously been depressed, elated, confused, determined, panic-stricken, privileged, numb and hopeless. If my tone wanders from technical to bossy, from stating the patently obvious to the downright cross, I apologize here and now. I have become an 'eco worrier', but worrying is no bad thing when it comes to saving our environment.

If you have flicked through this book, looking at the beautiful photographs, reading a paragraph here and there, you might find yourself a little perplexed to find a recipe for strawberry jam alongside a lecture on saving the world from global warming. But I do believe that global warming, living wholesomely, awareness of the environment, respecting nature and using the gifts we have on our doorstep is one story. I don't advocate turning our backs on science in favour of scientifically unproven herbal remedies, and I don't expect everyone to become self sufficient. I do believe, however, that we should pay more attention to how our food is grown and where it comes from, what goes into our medicines, and the effect chemical cleaning materials are having on our health and environment.

SMALL CHANGES, BIG REWARDS

In 1987 the world began living beyond its sustainable means. We have used up our 'ecological budget' for 2007 two months early. Our ecological credit card is over its limit and the interest is in overdrive. Just as 'every little helps' when climbing out of the financial debt mire, every individual making small changes will start to clear this terrible, world-changing, debt.

This is a guide to changing your entire way of life. Just as important as how to make raspberry cordial, making the most of the fruits that come once a year, is to be aware of the non-toxic solutions you can use to clean up the kitchen afterwards. This is not a guide to sacrifice and hardship; on the contrary, it is a guide to embracing the gifts we have with great pleasure.

If, in years to come, it is established that there was nothing we could have done to prevent global warming, the suggestions in this book can do no harm. If, however, in future we see that together we all made a huge difference to climate change and the disasters it might have caused, then we can congratulate ourselves on a job well done. We will be the beneficiaries of a world with a healthy population where fairness is the embodiment of ecological politics, and safety is at the heart of farming and manufacturing.

Preparing your own cleaning products and growing your own organic fruit and vegetables is a safer, more ecologically sound way of living. This guide will hopefully encourage more people to see the damage we are doing to the environment by relying on carbon fuels, chemicals and fertilizers to sustain our lifestyle. It is possible to keep a clean house and maintain a fertile garden organically, to shop locally and seasonally, and to recycle and re-use as much as we possibly can. This way of life may sometimes be more time consuming but, having tried and tested all the recipes in this book, I have found that it is more efficient and ultimately much simpler and less stressful. Add to that the fact that you will save money, the environment and miles travelled, and this can only be a good thing.

Life in the twenty-first century

Our lives have changed immeasurably during the past century and life has become so much easier, richer, and more comfortable for those of us lucky enough to be born in the affluent, developed parts of the world.

We have become fatter, lazier, more tired, more stressed and more dependent on mood-altering/enhancing concoctions. We demand instant cures for the ills we find ourselves suffering from, be it antibiotics for a slight cough or outrageously expensive preparations which promise us

that they will prevent old age becoming visible on our faces. Our homes can be sparkling clean and germ free with the thousands of cleaning products served to us, as it were, on a nice clean plate. Life has become terribly, terribly easy. This clean and easy way of life is having a huge impact on our lives and environment. It is, quite literally, making us and our world very, very ill.

During the past 100 years scientists, doctors, industrialists, farmers and governments have developed cures for our ailments and solutions to all our needs. Governments and food suppliers – always under pressure to meet the demand for cheap food – have responded with the help of science and air miles. We believed that they knew best and we were grateful for their expert knowledge. In fairness, we have, as they say, never had it so good, but at what cost? It was accepted as good practice to feed brains and spinal cords to herbivores to increase their growth rate, thereby increasing profit and reducing the need for the green fields upon which they would naturally graze. DDT, banned in 1973, was once universally accepted as an effective and safe pesticide. Antibiotics and growth hormones are still routinely given to farm animals. Organically reared livestock survive and thrive without.

We have all lived through food scares and epidemics. Largely to blame are murky regulations and badly enforced laws on animal husbandry, poor food safety, manufacturing and production. There is no universal regime for imported foodstuffs requiring them to demonstrate high standards of animal husbandry or to be labelled with information concerning provenance. Look back at the lives of our forefathers who worked with nature and had the expertise to be self sufficient. Living organically and self sufficiently need not preclude importing from other countries, but it does mean that should the necessity arise, we would be capable of survival without outside help.

We have expended such energy on fighting Mother Nature in the name of progress and protecting ourselves from her tantrums that we forget to feel gratitude for her bounty. The time has come to stop and smell the roses, to take stock of the damage we have done and are doing, and quietly, gently, wisely alter our habits.

> '*You can shove nature out with a pitchfork,*
> *but she'll keep coming back.*'
>
> Traditional proverb

There is a great deal that we can do to make the world a better place. We are all aware of the impending disasters awaiting us if we continue on the path we are taking. The time will come, I feel sure, when the extravagance and unconsidered comfort we have grown to expect will become a thing of the past. We are so unaware of how our cheap food is produced it is terribly easy to throw away almost half of what we buy. In order to understand the real value of food, we need to consider our wasteful nature, pay fair rewards to farmers for their labours and support them by shopping locally and seasonally.

Growing one's own fruit and vegetables certainly encourages frugality, deference and pride. Apart from the immense pleasure it gives, knowing how to grow food is, I feel, something that is becoming increasingly important. It is good to know the cost of food, but better still to know its value.

The most wholesome path to take in preventing the global warming catastrophe before it is too late is to stop accepting the unacceptable. In this book I hope to enlighten you on how to lead life in a more thoughtful, careful, organic and ecologically friendly way. It is unlikely that many of us have the wherewithal to take on governments or food suppliers. However, it is within the scope of every one of us to vote with our wallet and custom, to protect ourselves and our families, to take charge of every molecule we ingest and every product we buy. As I write, I am aware that big business is investing in the organic revolution, presumably directed by market forces. Consumers are demanding good, honest, natural products from ecologically sensitive and sound, sustainable sources.

Working with nature

The most important and potentially life-saving gift we can give to our children is to teach them to have respect for, and to be aware of, the life-giving properties and life-enhancing nature of … nature. Learning to respect and nurture the land is a good start to understanding the importance of organic practices in the home and in the garden. The Soil Association is campaigning to educate our children by organizing farm visits so that they can learn about safe and wholesome farming methods.

Straight from the horse's mouth, so to speak, they will see how food is grown and processed by organic methods. Strong emphasis is placed on protecting the environment by adopting organic practices.

'Anyone whose heart is in the right place understands that organic by neglect is far different than organic by design.'

Joel Salatin

Both on farms and in our own gardens, the starting point for producing good, healthy food will always be a healthy, balanced, living soil. By now we have learnt that the chemicals and toxic compounds – used freely in combating weeds and pests, to fertilize and increase yields – often ultimately reveal themselves in the end to be dangerous to wildlife and humans alike. Their persistence in the soil is still an unknown quantity for many of them and the exact effect of certain chemicals on humans and their offspring is still in debate. By contrast, organic methods have been tried and tested, and although, more often than not, to produce an entirely organic food requires more time and effort, at least we know what we are doing to our soil, our food and the wildlife that we all depend upon.

Where organic farmers lead, organic gardeners follow. But not all farming practices work on the vegetable plot, as I was intrigued to learn on a visit

to an organic vegetable farm. Extensive rows of perfectly formed cabbages spread out into the distance, not one blemish or hole was visible, the familiar lacey bug-infected leaves nowhere to be seen. There were no pests and no damage to the large, healthy leaves. The secret was revealed to me in a tone a child might use when explaining something patently obvious to a grown-up. Because there are no chemical fertilizers and no sprays used to rid the crop of insects, the natural balance of nature was allowed to set up home, and in moved the ladybirds, hedgehogs and birds, all of whom feast upon the insects attracted to the crop – a simple solution with no resulting problems. Protecting home-grown crops is not quite so easy, but methods to encourage wildlife and to extinguish pests are explained in Chapter 5.

*'The only thing that can save the world is the reclaiming
of the awareness of the world.'*

Allen Ginsberg

Change your lifestyle today

Scientists predict that, unless we reduce our impact on the environment NOW, the damage will be irreversible. We are in a perilous state and unless we all react and understand the situation TODAY, we will be leaving our children and our grandchildren a world of chaos, catastrophe and disaster –

we cannot guarantee that Mother Nature will look after them. If we are behaving in a greedy and reckless way, the first step to solving the problem is recognizing the fact. The second step is to do something about it. You have bought this book and, hopefully, it will make a small difference in your life and a huge difference to the world as we know it.

I am not an authority on housekeeping, gardening, weather patterns, animal husbandry or science. I know almost nothing about the scientific reasons for global warming and have not the least idea about why we are allowing our governments to get away with NOT DOING VERY MUCH AT ALL ABOUT IT. However, I am a mother and hopefully one day I shall be a grandmother. My publishers have been kind enough to ask me to do this book and if it changes 20 lives, or reduces 100lbs of carbon footprint it will have been worth the effort. If it introduces 50 more people to the ethics that Cabbages & Roses aspires to, or makes our little company just a bit richer so that we can afford to take our first steps to becoming completely organic, then I shall be happy.

This book is a guide to keeping your house clean by making your own cleaning preparations, growing your own produce and making your own remedies for minor complaints, with the emphasis on doing all these things organically. It encourages us to shop locally, seasonally and sustainably, supporting farmers and independent shopkeepers. If we all adopt this lifestyle, it will have a huge impact on our planet – that of being gentle with it. I have only included the tasks that I perform every year, every month or every day in this book. None of it is rocket science, but looking at my rituals, my survival techniques and methods of 'let's just see if it works', I feel rather pleased that I have learnt how to feed myself, clean myself and heal myself … organically.

My home is not particularly clean, and the dog and cats live in the kitchen. I am not obsessed with a germ-free environment and perhaps it is for this reason that my family is healthy. My garden is doing its best to provide the house with cut flowers, fruit and vegetables. Even so, I can now see that I must completely change the way I live in order to appease Mother Nature and encourage her to keep her temper and feed my grandchildren.

This book is a very simple, pared-down version of all those many expert books on adopting a self-sufficient, organic lifestyle. It is for survival in a greener and more wholesome way. There is enough information to start you on your way and to inspire you to do better, to be better and to live a better life on a healthier planet.

'We have to move away from a dumb economy that chews up, spits out and destroys nature and people, towards a smart one that operates with natural cycles: we need to learn to live within our limits.'

Dame Anita Roddick

CHAPTER 1

KEEPING HOUSE

In 2003 Greenpeace initiated a 'Chemical Home' database. Its aim was to demonstrate that it was possible to substitute hazardous chemicals in cleaning materials with safer alternatives. By 2006 many manufacturers had indeed found effective and safer alternatives, but there is still a long way to go. In this chapter you will find truly magical alternative cleaning materials, none of which will harm the environment, and all of which are cheap and – most importantly – extremely effective.

Our predilection for chemical anti-bacterial formulae and over-fastidiousness in our homes is, in my opinion, the reason for our seemingly weakened immune systems – I do believe your house can be too clean. Even if you choose to be obsessively clean, try the non-chemical approach for a while and delight in the absence of toxic cleaning materials, on which we all spend too much money and which are really not necessary at all.

Cleaning without chemicals

I have a rather casual approach to keeping house (which doesn't please my mother!) but whether or not I am tidy (not at all), where it matters I do make an effort. This is especially true where food hygiene is concerned – this is one area in my life where I am slightly obsessive (my children mock me).

I rather like cleaning – I am not very good at it, but find it both therapeutic and satisfying. As I am not as fastidious as I perhaps ought to be, this is definitely a book of 'do as I say' or 'do as I have recently learned', rather than 'do as I do'!

There is little in life more satisfying than tackling a really untidy, unclean room. Starting with the kitchen, I have been finding new ways of dealing with problems that seemed insoluble when all I had to rely on were chemical concoctions that promised to work wonders. In fact some – most – really don't.

This is by no means a comprehensive advisory chapter on how to keep your house clean. It is merely a hint as to how, by using very few cleaning products, most household chores can be achieved simply, effectively, non-toxically and safely. I have not covered specialized subjects such as how to dust the frames of priceless paintings (vacuum, covering the nozzle with fine gauze), or how to clean finely carved antique furniture (remove dust with a clean soft paintbrush and use natural beeswax, not aerosol spray polish). This is just a very simple, ordinary, day-to-day list of general housekeeping equipment, cleaning products and techniques.

DISPOSABLE WIPES
These wipes are not environmentally friendly. Use them only in emergency situations, perhaps keeping a packet in the car. The rest of the time water and cloth will do the same job – on picnics, for example, take a glass bottle of water and some recycled cloths with you.

RIGHT: *With only two vital cleaning products required for most household tasks, they can be kept easily accessible.*

The cleaning cupboard

This is a list of the housekeeping equipment and cleaning products that I find useful. I have no need for anything more – mine is a small but friendly cleaning-product cupboard. I lead a small but friendly life!

Beeswax polish (see page 32)

Bicarbonate of soda, in industrial quantities (see pages 28–30)

Borax (see page 32)

Chamois leather, for cleaning windows and rubbing off pet hair

Distilled white vinegar, in industrial quantities (see pages 22–27)

Natural, ready-prepared cleaning fluids and washing powder (such as Ecover)

Enamel buckets – a good selection, preferably vintage. Why buy new ones when there are so many available from flea markets and junk shops?

Feather or lambswool duster with a long handle for reaching cobwebs and behind furniture

Jam jars with screw lids

Lemons, for various cleaning purposes

Muslin, for food covers, straining jelly, etc.

Old toothbrushes, for cleaning awkward corners

Rags, for use as cleaning cloths. Make these from worn-out cotton frocks and T-shirts, towels, tea towels, and sheets and pillowcases that are beyond mending. Cut the cloth into squares, then wash or boil your used rags regularly. You may never need to buy another duster again – most people have enough fabric waste to last them a lifetime.

Refillable spray bottles

Soda crystals

Washing line and wooden pegs

Wooden bristle scrubbing brush

Wooden-handled, bristle-brushed brooms (these last forever, unlike their plastic counterparts). A hard-bristle brush is best for outdoor use and a soft-bristle brush for indoor sweeping.

Wooden-handled, small bristle brush with tin dustpan (plastic is not eco-friendly and does not last as it is breakable). As above, a soft-bristle brush is best for indoors while a hard-bristle brush removes dried mud and other dirt from carpets and rugs.

LEFT: *Jam jars with screw lids and kilner jars are useful for all manner of things, from home-made jam to storing dusters dipped in lemon oil, or for keeping leftovers in the fridge.*

lemon dusters

Whether you are using bought dusters or cutting up old cotton clothes, towels or tea towels to serve the purpose, with this method you can clean your furniture without resorting to spray polish. Prepare several dusters at a time and store until needed. Make sure you wash or boil the dusters regularly after use and re-infuse them with lemon and oil.

you will need
Water
White distilled vinegar
Lemon oil or olive oil
Dusters or rags
Lemons
Airtight jar with screw lid

1 Make a solution of two parts water, two parts vinegar and two drops of lemon oil or olive oil. Soak your dusters or rags in this solution and squeeze out the excess, leaving them just damp.

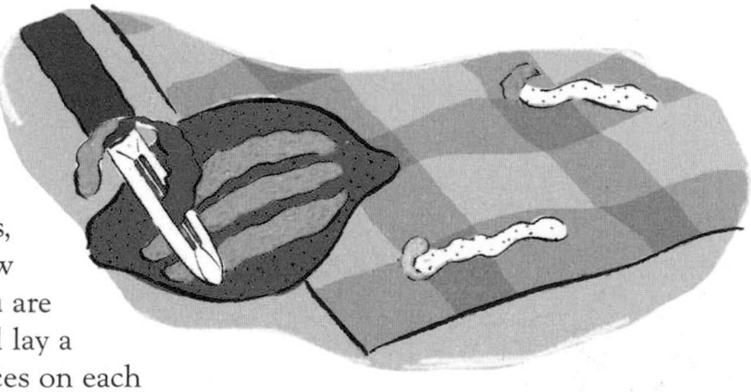

2 Pare the rind from several lemons, depending how many rags you are preparing, and lay a couple of pieces on each smoothed-out duster.

3 Fold each one, or roll it up, and store in a clean jam jar with an extra piece of lemon peel. The jar should be airtight with a screw lid.

White distilled vinegar

For 10,000 years this fermented alcohol (most probably accidentally stumbled upon) has had hundreds of different uses. The Babylonians discovered its preserving properties, while the Romans drank it, the Greeks pickled vegetables and meats in it, and soldiers during the US Civil War used it to treat scurvy. It heals wounds, cleans glass and melts away limescale and grease.

For the recipes in this chapter use only white distilled vinegar – once you realize how useful it is, you will probably want to stock up on several gallons of this magical liquid!

Altered hem and seam lines

If you mind about holes left after taking down a hem or re-sewing a seam, iron the fabric over a cloth dampened with vinegar.

Baby clothes

To freshen baby clothes, add one cup of vinegar to the detergent dispenser of the washing machine for the final rinse cycle. This will break down the uric acid and soapy residue on the clothes, leaving them soft and fresh. (You may also want to do this to liven up tired fabrics.)

Blankets

To wash wool or cotton blankets, add two cups of vinegar to the rinse cycle. This will make them soft, fluffy and free of soap.

Boiled eggs

To prevent an egg from leaking from its shell while it is being boiled, add a splash of vinegar to the water.

LEFT: *Adding a drop of vinegar to the cooking water will stop eggshells leaking.*

RIGHT: *Keep a permanent washing line strung up in a spare room or laundry and use it to dry clothes when the weather is inclement.*

Brass, copper and pewter

To make an effective polish, mix one teaspoon of salt and one cup of vinegar, stirring in enough flour to make a paste. Cover the item with the paste and leave for 15 minutes. Wash off with warm water and polish with a soft dry cloth.

Burn marks

Rub neat vinegar onto the fabric with a soft cloth, then rinse with water. (Test on a non-conspicuous area first.)

Carpet stains

Blot spills as soon as possible with a kitchen towel. For a stain, mix one teaspoon of Ecover washing-up liquid with one teaspoon of vinegar dissolved in one pint (just over half a litre) of lukewarm water. Apply to the stain with a soft cloth and rub gently. Rinse with warm water and blot dry.

Cigarette odours

To remove the odour of cigar or cigarette smoke, leave a saucer of vinegar in the room overnight.

Cooking odours

To rid the kitchen of cooking odours, simmer a solution of vinegar and water in a pan for 5 minutes.

Cut flowers

To keep cut flowers fresh for longer, add two teaspoons of sugar and two tablespoons of vinegar to the flower water. Trim the stems and change the water every five days.

Deodorant stains

To remove deodorant stains on coloured clothes, rub with a soft cloth dipped in vinegar and wash as usual.

LEFT: *Keep glossy copper pots in prime condition by cleaning with a paste made from vinegar, salt and flour.*

Drains

To deodorize drains, pour a cup of vinegar down the drain and leave for half an hour, then flush through with running cold water. A mixture of vinegar and bicarbonate of soda will do the job even more thoroughly. Pour two tablespoons of bicarbonate of soda down the plug hole followed by half a cup of vinegar, leave to bubble for 20 minutes, then flush through by running the cold tap for a minute.

Dyeing fabric

When dyeing fabrics, add a tablespoon of vinegar to the final rinse to help set the colour.

Fish

When steaming, poaching or baking fish, soak it in vinegar and water for half an hour before cooking. This will keep the flesh from crumbling and make it tender and sweeter to taste. Rinse in cold water before cooking.

Fruit stains on hands

Clean fruit-stained hands with neat vinegar.

Insect pests

If you have trouble with insects (silver fish, ants etc.) wipe down kitchen surfaces with neat vinegar to deter visits. This will also disinfect the surfaces.

Iron plate stains

Mix one part vinegar with one part salt and heat gently in a small pan. Rub the solution onto the cold iron plate to remove stains. Wipe clean with a damp cloth.

Lavatory bowl staining

To freshen up the lavatory and remove stubborn stains, spray neat vinegar around the bowl and brush clean. Leave to soak overnight if necessary.

RIGHT: *Vintage linen tea towels can be soaked in vinegar and water to remove stains and lengthen their life.*

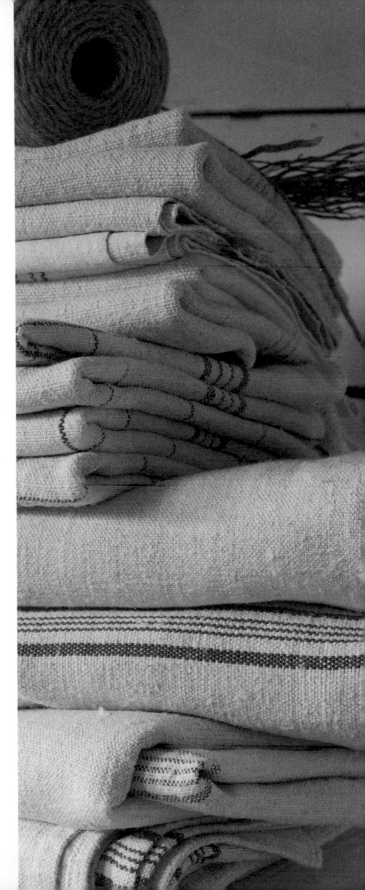

Leather

Mix one part vinegar with two parts linseed oil then use a soft cloth to rub the solution into the leather. Buff with a clean cloth. (Test on a non-conspicuous area first.)

Limescale in showerhead

If the showerhead is clogged with limescale, soak in a bowl of one part vinegar to three parts water. Check after 30 minutes and rinse in clean cold water.

Limescale on taps

To rid taps of limescale build-up, soak a towelling rag in vinegar, then wrap it around the taps and areas of build-up. Leave for half an hour, then rinse clean.

Microwave ovens

To clean and deodorize a microwave oven, fill a microwaveable bowl with vinegar and boil in the oven. This will loosen dried food on the walls, which can then be wiped clean with a soft damp cloth.

Paint brushes

To soften stiff paint brushes, soak the bristles in hot vinegar. Rinse with clean, soapy water before using.

Painted walls and woodwork

Make a solution of two parts vinegar, one part bicarbonate of soda and three parts warm water. Dip a soft cloth into the solution and use it to wipe the dirt from surfaces, then rinse with clean water.

Potatoes

To keep peeled potatoes white, add a teaspoon of vinegar to the water they are soaking in until they are cooked.

Red wine stains

Blot the stain immediately with a soft, dry cloth, and sponge with undiluted vinegar until it is gone.

Refrigerators

Clean the inside of the refrigerator with a solution made from equal parts of vinegar and water.

Ring marks on wooden furniture

To remove ring marks on wooden furniture, make a solution of one part vinegar and one part olive oil. Use a soft cloth to rub the ring mark with the solution, then polish with natural beeswax.

Rinsing fresh produce

To freshen salads and vegetables, or to clean chemical residue from shop-bought non-organic fresh produce, soak in cold water to which you have added two tablespoons of vinegar. Rinse after soaking.

LEFT: *Wooden chopping boards will last much longer than a lifetime. Lemons will clean and disinfect them.*

Rust stains

Remove rust stains on delicate fabrics with a mixture of vinegar and hot water. Dab the spot gently with the solution on a clean cloth until the rust is removed. (Another traditional method of removing rust stains or iron mould from delicate fabrics is to soak the item in the juice of cooked rhubarb, then rinse in clean warm water.)

Sink waste disposal units

To clean a sink waste disposal unit, make ice cubes with one part vinegar and one part water. Put the cubes into the unit and switch on. This spatters the vinegar cubes throughout the system. Flush the unit with cold water afterwards.

Stale odours

To remove stale odours lurking in biscuit tins or lunch boxes, dip a slice of fresh bread in vinegar and leave in the tin or box overnight.

Steam irons

To remove limescale from steam irons, mix equal quantities of vinegar and distilled water and fill the water chamber. Heat the iron for 5 minutes, then press the steam button over scrap fabric to rid the chamber of limescale. When cool, tip out the solution. Rinse the chamber well.

Windows

Make a solution of one part vinegar and one part warm water. Pour into a spray bottle, then spray onto glass. Rub the glass dry with a soft cloth, then polish with crumpled newspaper for a sheen.

Wooden chopping boards

Vinegar or lemon juice will clean, deodorize and disinfect wooden chopping boards. These are naturally more hygienic and more ecologically sound than the plastic varieties.

RIGHT: *Windows can be made sparklingly clear with just vinegar and old newspaper.*

Bicarbonate of soda

This is another miracle of nature. Most bicarbonate of soda is made from trona ore, mined from natural deposits throughout the world, but predominantly found in Wyoming, USA. Bicarbonate of soda can be manufactured and is formed by combining carbonic acid and sodium hydroxide. Trona, however, is a naturally occurring substance that is easily mined, and it is the source of most bicarbonate of soda.

Trona was discovered in the mid 1840s. Then, as now, it was used by many households for scouring, cleaning and deodorizing. Trona is also known as baking soda, bicarbonate of soda and sodium bicarbonate. It is best known for its uses in cooking, becoming a rising agent when it is mixed with cream of tartar.

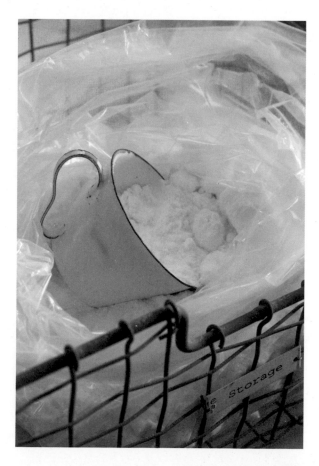

Brass
To clean brass, make a paste of bicarbonate of soda and lemon juice. Apply and leave for a minute before rinsing well.

Carpets
Sprinkle bicarbonate of soda over carpets to deodorize them. Leave for an hour, then vacuum.

Chrome
For polishing chrome, make a paste of bicarbonate of soda and water. Rinse thoroughly with clean water to remove deposits.

Cooking cabbage
To keep cabbage bright green during cooking, add a pinch of bicarbonate of soda to the water. This helps the leaves to retain their magnesium.

Cut flowers
Add a pinch of bicarbonate of soda to cut flower water to keep it fresher for longer. This works as well as the sugar and vinegar solution (see page 24).

Dish cloths and flannels
Soak dish cloths and face flannels in a strong solution of bicarbonate of soda and water to freshen them up.

Dustbins
Sprinkle bicarbonate of soda into the bottom of dustbins to remove unpleasant odours. After emptying the rubbish, add some water and swill around the dustbin. Pour it out and leave to dry, then add more bicarbonate of soda for next time.

LEFT: *Use bicarbonate of soda instead of a multitude of chemical cleaning products.*

RIGHT: *Cut flowers will last longer if a pinch of bicarb is dissolved in the water.*

Glass decanters

To clean the hard-to-reach inside of a glass decanter, make a solution of bicarbonate of soda, crushed dry eggshells and warm water. Swish around in the decanter and leave overnight. Rinse well with white distilled vinegar to remove the residue, then rinse thoroughly with warm water.

Hairbrushes and combs

Make a solution of bicarbonate of soda and warm water. Soak hairbrushes and combs for an hour to remove dirt and grease, then rinse with warm water.

Kitchens and bathrooms

When mixed with water, bicarbonate of soda makes an alkaline solution that will cut through grease and dirt on most surfaces in kitchens and bathrooms. Used dry, it is effective as an abrasive powder; mixed with distilled white vinegar it becomes even more powerful.

Laundry

To reduce the amount of washing powder used for each laundry load and to make it more effective, substitute half the normal dose with bicarbonate of soda. (Washing powder contains far fewer chemicals than its liquid equivalents.)

Mattress stains

To remove mattress stains, make a loose paste of bicarbonate of soda and water and apply to the stain. Leave to dry so that the powder disperses into the mattress, then brush it off. The bicarbonate of soda will also deodorize the mattress.

Mildew on shower curtains

To remove mildew growing on shower curtains, apply a paste of bicarbonate of soda and water. Leave on the curtain overnight and wash off the next day with warm water.

Oven cleaning

After cleaning the oven, make a light paste of bicarbonate of soda and water. Use it to brush inside the oven and you will find that cleaning is much easier next time.

Refrigerator odours

Keep a saucer of bicarbonate of soda inside the fridge to absorb and remove food odours, replacing it every two weeks. And instead of throwing away the old bicarbonate of soda, pour it into the kitchen sink followed by a kettle of boiling water to keep drains fresh and odour-free.

Rust on cooking utensils

Dip the cut edge of a potato into a saucer of bicarbonate of soda and rub over the rust. Rinse the utensil, then wipe it with a cloth dipped in a little olive oil to prevent the rust from forming again.

Silver

To clean silver, soak it in boiling water with bicarbonate of soda, cream of tartar, salt and a piece of aluminium foil.

Stains inside cups and teapots

Fill the items with a solution of bicarbonate of soda and water. Leave until the staining disappears, then rinse. For stubborn stains, use a solution of bicarbonate of soda and white distilled vinegar.

RIGHT: *A tried-and-tested method for cleaning glass decanters is to use a mixture of crushed eggshells, bicarbonate of soda and warm water.*

Borax

An extremely effective anti-bacterial, fungicidal cleaning and bleaching agent, borax is almost as effective as normal commercial bleach. It is, however, a healthier option for the environment. It has low toxicity for people, though higher toxicity for animals.

Carpet stains

Mix the borax with a little water into a paste. Test on an unexposed area of carpet for colour fastness then rub into the stain, allow to dry and vacuum off the powder. For wine and other liquid stains, dissolve half a cup of borax in half a litre (about quarter of a pint) of warm water. Rub into the stain, leave for 30 minutes and sponge off. For odours, dampen the area, sprinkle with borax, leave to dry then vacuum.

Laundry

Add half a cup of borax to your wash load with the usual amount of washing powder to boost its cleaning power and deodorize the wash.

Refrigerators

Dissolve one tablespoon of borax in a litre (about half a pint) of warm water and use to wipe the fridge clean and deodorize it at the same time.

Washing delicates

Soak in a solution of half a cup of borax with one or two tablespoons of washing powder in a bowl of warm water. Rinse in cool water and dry as appropriate.

Beeswax

Making your own beeswax polish is simple, but potentially very dangerous as the ingredients – pure beeswax and turpentine – are extremely flammable. They do not boil but become hotter and hotter until they catch fire. The flash point is low. Like chip-pan fires, burning beeswax is particularly difficult to extinguish. This is why I suggest you buy natural beeswax polish instead of making it.

For cleaning wood furniture, beeswax is infinitely preferable to the polish sold in aerosol cans and containing silicone. Spray polishes create a shiny, impenetrable surface whereas beeswax feeds the wood, giving it a luxurious, deep, well-fed shine. It is not necessary to polish furniture more than about four or five times a year, provided it is kept dusted. (For intricately carved pieces of furniture or picture frames, a soft, fat, clean paintbrush can be used to remove dust from tricky corners.) An alternative to beeswax is a drop of olive oil. This will feed the wood and, when buffed up with a soft cloth, produce a lovely natural shine.

RIGHT: *Use a vintage enamel pail to soak delicate items in a solution of borax and warm water.*

Kitchen hygiene

All kitchen surfaces and wooden chopping boards should be kept as clean as possible, using any of the ingredients listed on pages 22–32 or ecologically safe and sound brands.

I feel our dependence on anti-bacterial substances has made us a tad lazy in the kitchen hygiene department. It is not necessary to rely on chemicals to keep our kitchens clean and to avoid food poisoning. Common sense and an awareness of the dangers contained in raw meat, fish and some other foods should keep you and your family safe and healthy. Thorough cooking of foods at high enough temperatures, cleanliness, hand washing and the avoidance of cross contamination are all essential if you are to avoid causing illness.

Wash hands and surfaces thoroughly after handling raw meat, and keep all raw meats on a covered plate at the bottom of the refrigerator.

Dry your hands on a towel kept purely for that purpose and do not be tempted to use the same towel to dry dishes. Change dish cloths and tea towels every day. Keep them clean by boiling them regularly in a solution of water and white distilled vinegar with a teaspoon of bicarbonate of soda. This is especially important after using them with raw meat and fish.

RIGHT: *Keep separate towels for drying hands and dishes, to avoid any cross contamination.*

Chopping boards

Although we were led to believe that plastic boards were safer than their wooden counterparts, research carried out by microbiologists at the University of Wisconsin's Food Research Institute in 1993 proved otherwise. Testing the theory that wood contained anti-bacterial properties, in a controlled experiment they intentionally contaminated both types of chopping board with bacteria responsible for food poisoning. Their study showed that germs placed on the wooden chopping board died within three minutes but the bacteria on the plastic board not only remained alive but multiplied overnight.

The explanation for these incredible results is that wood has natural anti-bacterial properties. The capillary action of dry wood means that germs disappear quickly beneath the surface of the board where they soon die, leaving the exposed dry area free from microbes. In contrast, the smooth impenetrable surface of the plastic board hosted germs comfortably. Where the board has been scarred by knives, the germs are there to stay and multiply.

In spite of these findings, it is important that you never assume that wooden chopping boards decontaminate themselves. Hand washing or scrubbing both types of boards thoroughly with soap and hot water (if you insist on using a plastic board, here is one situation where I would excuse the use of anti-bacterial soap) will probably kill most dangerous germs. However, where raw chicken is concerned, I would go so far as scrubbing with soap and boiling water.

To disinfect both wooden and plastic boards, spray first with white distilled vinegar, then spray with hydrogen peroxide. This combination will kill bacteria. Keep chopping boards dry when not in use as bacteria do not survive more than a few hours without moisture.

Some manufacturers claim that their anti-bacterial plastic chopping boards are self-sanitizing. These claims are untrue – it is not possible to produce plastic that is inherently anti-bacterial.

In short, opt for our grandmothers' choice of chopping board – good old-fashioned wood, scrubbed clean with a bristle brush. A sensible precaution is to keep boards used for bread and vegetables separate from those used for meat.

RIGHT: *This glass cover is beautiful enough for the table. A wire dome covering is also extremely practical, allowing air to circulate but keeping flies away.*

BELOW: *Have plenty of wooden chopping boards, and make sure all members of the household know which to use just for meat.*

Food covers

In order to research the safety of cling film, I contacted the United Kingdom's Food Standards Agency. Their website advises that cling film is safe if used correctly, and that not every cling film is safe for all uses. They recommend the following points, which are aimed at protecting the quality and taste of food from easily avoidable migration from cling films, and preventing inappropriate use of films:

- Do not use cling films where they may melt into the food, such as in conventional ovens or with pots and pans on cooker hobs.
- When re-heating or cooking food in a microwave oven, ensure that the cling film does not touch the food.

- Only use cling film in contact with high fat foods when the manufacturer's advice states it is suitable for this. Examples of high fat foods include some types of cheese, raw meats with a layer of fat, fried meats, pastry products, and cakes with butter icing or chocolate coatings.

My opinion is that, if it is necessary for a product to carry any sort of warning at all, it should be avoided. While the United Kingdom's Food Standards Agency states that cling film is safe when used correctly, I can only presume that it is not safe when used incorrectly. I contacted the Agency to enquire exactly what the effects and/or dangers are in using cling film on certain types of food. Their reply simply reiterated the instruction to avoid using cling film with fatty foods. When pressed on the point, the Agency advisor could/would not expand on what harm is done by inappropriate use of cling film. I was assured that by law all packaging of cling film had to carry a warning.

My concern is that while warnings provide protection for the manufacturer, it is unlikely that most of the population will ever feel it necessary to read instructions on something as seemingly benign as cling film. Common sense dictates that food should be covered, but it is debatable whether cling film is the right kind of covering to use.

Alternative food covers
Infinitely preferable to cling film are re-useable food covers. There is a multitude of options, including wire, netting, glass and fabric – simple muslin is something often forgotten about. An upturned plate will suffice for cooling a dish before putting it into the fridge. And don't forget about using good old-fashioned greaseproof paper, particularly for wrapping sandwiches – string or an elastic band will keep it in place.

'Sell-by' dates are for the
guidance of sellers ONLY.
'Use-by' dates are for us, the
consumers

Sell-by dates

I cannot imagine how much profit is made by supermarkets and food producers from 'sell-by dates'. I am guilty of blindly following date guidance because I am from a generation that has always believed that big business knows best. While I cannot categorically say that sell-by dates are a bad thing, it is a convenient and slightly sneaky way to encourage people to dispose of and buy more food. For some time (most of my adult life actually) I have erred on the side of caution rather than using my own natural senses, instinct and sense of self-preservation. Yet by using your sense of smell, your eyesight and by buying from suppliers you trust, you will save a fortune by not throwing away food merely because the packaging tells you to do so.

BELOW: *Before using eggs in your recipes, check their freshness by seeing if they sink in a glass of water.*

Determining food freshness

Eggs One thing that is often difficult to judge by its 'use-by' date is an egg. A simple test for freshness is to place the egg in a glass of water. If it sinks to the bottom of the glass, it is fresh enough to use, but if it floats, do not use it.

Don't keep eggs in the fridge.

Fruit and vegetables Provided that they are not excessively packaged, it is simple to determine the freshness of fruit and vegetables. They should be firm and brightly coloured. If they are not of perfect shape or have slight blemishes, use your common sense to judge whether they are edible or not. Sadly, we have been dictated to by nonsensical laws governing the suitable shape of our vegetables – a bent carrot or a straight banana will have no relevance to its taste or freshness.

Cut any bruises etc out and use the rest.

Local suppliers Meats – cooked or not – should be bought from a reputable supplier. Get to know your butcher/your local delicatessen/your cheese shop. Judge their hygiene standards by your own. If they sell you produce that is disappointing/poisonous/delicious, let them know. By building up a relationship with your shopkeepers everybody wins – not only does shopping become more of a pleasure, but the social interaction (which has been lost to the faceless and homogenized atmosphere of the supermarket) can also be reinstated.

Recycling in the kitchen

As much as you can, try to avoid buying food that has been excessively packaged. This is much simpler if you shop locally, at farmers' markets or specialist food shops. If you do find yourself in a supermarket, opt for loose vegetables rather than the pre-packaged varieties that come in polystyrene trays covered with impossible-to-unwrap plastic, then sold in a plastic bag.

Avoid using plastic bags by always having a re-usable cloth shopping bag folded in your handbag, or keep a good supply of them in the car. We all managed perfectly well before plastic carrier bags were invented by using baskets, string bags, wheelie shopping bags and cardboard boxes. We used to save brown paper carrier bags, wrapping paper and brown paper, folded neatly and ready to be reused. Cardboard boxes used to be readily available in supermarkets, but I haven't seen them for a good long while.

All these things are a good alternative to the mountains of plastic we have come to rely on.

RIGHT: *Baskets and fabric shoppers are preferable to, and much more beautiful than, plastic carrier bags.*

Reducing packaging

Buy in bulk wherever possible and you can avoid having to throw away at least half of the usual amount of packaging used for smaller units. If you have the space to store dry goods that won't deteriorate with age (such as lavatory paper, distilled vinegar, bicarbonate of soda, borax, Epsom salts, washing powder), buy them in sufficient quantities to last three months. Having a stock of these bulky items makes food shopping not only more pleasurable, but possible to do on foot.

One of the few modern-day inventions that can make up for its carbon footprint in its usefulness is the freezer. Well stocked and efficiently run, it can save many a trip to the supermarket, and is invaluable for storing seasonal fruit and vegetables from the garden or market, to keep you fed throughout the winter months.

Council recycling schemes

Recycle glass, tins, foil and plastic, and compost all uncooked vegetable matter (see pages 72–77). Local councils offer recycling schemes, so contact them to find out how you should go about recycling. Certainly in the UK, the business of recycling has become rather complicated, frightening even with talk of cameras in dustbins, records kept of what we throw away and fines for the wrong type of rubbish.

If councils are truly concerned about recycling, they will make it simple for us to do . One clear rule throughout the country would be a good start. Tell us what to do and we will do it. Make it easy for us to do and we will do it with pleasure. Threaten us and, like children, we will dig our heels in and will not co-operate.

Recycled china

I can think of nothing prettier than a dresser full of mis-matched vintage china. I can think of little more dull than a dresser full of matching china. Not only is mis-matched china cheaper, more interesting and a beautiful exercise in recycling, it saves the problem of finding or replacing a piece of china from a discontinued range. If you start in a muddle, you can continue in a muddle and make a beautiful display of it.

Avoid buying cracked or chipped china if it is to be used in cooking or for food, but pieces that are less than perfect can be used as ashtrays, soap dishes or bowls for fragrant pot pourri. Cups can be filled with candle wax and given away as gifts (see page 176).

If you use a dishwasher, make sure that everyday china is dishwasher proof or you might find that the patterns fade to nothing over time. My vintage china is rarely used but when it is I wash it by hand.

Keep glass, both old and new, gleaming with recipes using vinegar and other concoctions listed on pages 18–20.

RIGHT: *Mis-matched china makes an interesting display on the open shelves of a kitchen dresser.*

Household pests

Every household has its share of uninvited visitors, especially if you have pets sharing your space. Our normal reaction is to turn to toxic commercial pesticides, which may well do more harm than good. Unless your problem is extreme, natural, non-toxic alternatives will deal with most problems.

Start by deterring pests from moving into your home in the first place. Seal cracks and holes and, if a hole is too inconvenient to fill, prevent rats and mice from entering by filling the gap with wire wool. This is one of the only materials that even rats won't bother to gnaw through. Humane traps are available that allow the rodent to be released into the wild. However, rats are quite a big pest to deal with so, personally, I would call in the professionals if you are unfortunate enough to have a problem.

Ants

If you are plagued with ants inside the house, the first thing to establish is where they are coming from and why. Remove the crumbs or food sources that are tempting them. Wipe surfaces with distilled white vinegar or pure lemon juice. At the point of entry lay any of the following deterrents: cayenne pepper; cinnamon; citrus oil; cloves; sliced cloves of fresh garlic; crushed dried lemon peel; lemon juice; dried mint leaves; and, curiously, cucumber peel.

Cockroaches

These unsightly creatures often live at high levels, so when using deterrents don't forget to spray above cupboards and shelves. Simmer catnip sachets in water to make a solution to spray on areas infested by cockroaches. They dislike soapy water so, if you do suffer an infestation in your home, keep a spray bottle filled with a strong solution of soap and water handy as this will kill them. Borax dissolved in water in a spray bottle will also kill these horrid pests. Other deterrents include bay leaves, garlic and sliced cucumber. Non-toxic cockroach traps are available .

KEEPING RODENTS AT BAY
Once a month use peppermint oil in your floor cleaning water to ward off rodents. Keep a refillable spray bottle filled with a strong mixture of water and peppermint oil to spray around the outside of dustbins, in attic spaces and the backs of cupboards.

PETS AND PESTS

Animal parasites

To deter ticks and fleas on cats and dogs, add about a teaspoon of vinegar to your pet's water bowl. As a guide, for an 18kg (40lb) creature (dog, not a flea!) add one teaspoon per approximately 1 litre (2 pints) of water.

Puppy accidents

To prevent puppy accidents from staining carpets, sprinkle with neat vinegar (test for colour fastness in an inconspicuous area) and blot with clean absorbent cloth or paper towel. Repeat if necessary. This treatment will also prevent odours.

Fleas on pets

These are a constant problem especially in the summer months. Adding distilled white vinegar or apple cider vinegar to your pet's drinking water will act as a deterrent. Washing pets regularly with mild soap to which you have added the juice of a lemon will also keep the little beasts at bay.

Dip a comb in a solution made from boiling water poured onto lemon slices, wait until cool, then comb your pet with the lemon water to act as a further deterrent. If you trap fleas on the comb, drown them in soapy water immediately by immersing the comb into a prepared bowl.

Cedar shampoo and cedar oil can also be used in the fight against flea infestation. Make a solution of water, vinegar and cedar oil. Keep this in a spray bottle and spray pet bedding regularly to keep fleas away. Make a pocket from muslin, fill it with a mixture of cedar chips, lavender and lemon peel, and place it under the bedding inside pet baskets. Change the mixture every month or so to keep it fresh and effective.

Keep carpets and areas under furniture well vacuumed and, if you know fleas have been present, empty the vacuum bag every time you use it, sealing and disposing of the contents carefully outside.

RIGHT: *It's far better to keep your pet pest-free by using natural remedies rather than harsh chemicals.*

Dust mites

This ever-present microscopic creature is not such a problem unless someone in your household has an allergic reaction or suffers from asthma. If so, seek medical advice, but really the only way to deal with mites is to be scrupulous with vacuuming. Pay special attention to mattresses, fabric-covered headboards and pillows. Keep furniture, books, throws and rugs dust-free by vacuuming. Seal the vacuum bag tightly and dispose of it carefully. If possible, air items and beat throws, blankets, duvets and rugs outside in the fresh air. Hang the items on a line outside and thwack – if you can't find a carpet beater, an old tennis racket is just as effective. Washing bedding regularly at 55 degrees should rid bedding of mites.

Mosquitoes

Mosquitoes are a horrible fact of life, especially if you live near still water. There are many commercial, non-toxic preparations available, but the following will also deter them.

Mix one part garlic juice with five parts water and keep in a spray bottle. Shake well before use, then spray onto exposed parts of the body. To prevent mosquitoes from entering the house, hang strips of cotton cloth dipped into this solution at open windows or, if you have gauze screens, spray these with the solution. For outside eating areas, surround the table with marigold, rosemary and sage plants. Avoid still water – bird baths, still ponds and puddles – near social areas. For sleeping, a mosquito net hung over the bed is the best natural deterrent available.

Moths

Once moths have set up home, it is extremely difficult to persuade them to leave. One of the best lines of defence is to be scrupulous in your vacuuming, paying special attention to the edges of rooms and underneath furniture and rugs. The second is to be extremely vigilant when buying old and imported furniture, rugs, natural floor coverings and second-hand or vintage clothing. These are often the origin of an infestation.

Natural moth deterrents include:

- aromatic cedar chips
- bay leaves
- dried lemon peel
- lavender
- rosemary
- rose petals

All these natural ingredients can be combined into an attractive, fragrant pot pourri (as the Elizabethans did) and displayed in bowls placed in strategic positions around the house. Alternatively, you can make muslin pockets, fill them with some of the ingredients and tie with string. Even having taken all precautions in avoidance of moths, vigilance is still the most important thing you can practise.

If you do find yourself with a moth problem, soak porous string in cedar, lavender or rosemary oil, then trail this around the edges of the room between the wall and the edge of the carpet. Make sure the string is not wet or saturated when you lay it as it may stain the carpet. Leave it to drip outside so that it is infused but not wet.

MOTH BALLS

Avoid chemically made moth balls as they contain naphthalene, which can be fatal to small children and pets. They also have a musty, unpleasant odour, which will permeate your clothes and be very difficult to get rid of.

FOOD MOTHS

These are found in dry goods such as flour and cereals. Like mice, they can chew their way into cardboard and paper packaging but, unlike mice, they are tiny and difficult to detect.

Make sure you clean out your larder regularly and vacuum the corners of the room where they are likely to be entering. Decant dry goods from packets into sealed containers and keep a watchful eye.

sticky fly paper

No need to kill any of these pests, Just deter them in the first place

These home-made concoctions are wonderful for trapping all types of flying insects and infinitely preferable to toxic fly sprays. The paper can be changed as soon as it becomes disturbingly full – a fly paper at full capacity is not an attractive sight.

Make several at a time and hang them strategically around the kitchen, or wherever you have a flying insect problem. A word of warning, though – do not make the mistake of hanging them where passing people might get their hair caught. I have known this to happen and I cannot think of anything worse than having this sticky contraption tangled in your hair!

you will need
Strong brown paper
Scissors
Hole puncher
String
Saucepan
Water
Sugar
Honey or golden syrup
Baking tray

1 Cut some strips of tough brown paper. Make a hole at the top of each strip so that you can thread a length of string through it to form a hanging loop.

2 In a saucepan, mix one part water, one part sugar and one part honey or golden syrup, and heat until the mixture has combined well. Turn off the heat and allow the mixture to cool a little.

3 Dip each paper strip into the syrup mixture, making sure each side is well coated.

4 Suspend the strips over a baking tray and leave to drip. When dry, the sticky fly papers are ready to hang up in place.

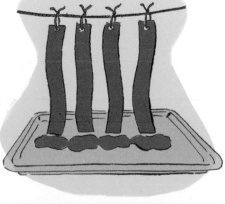

The wardrobe

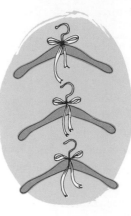

At the forefront of the news headlines in recent months is the exposure of unscrupulous manufacturers flouting employment laws and behaving in Machiavellian ways, paying low wages and sometimes no wages at all to the most vulnerable people in the workplace. Providing appalling working conditions, these manufacturers force unnaturally long hours on their workers and impose contracts that tie them to their workplace, sometimes for life. Children are among the most vulnerable, employed in factories where they work for as much as 10 hours a day, often in poorly ventilated and dangerous conditions.

According to the charity Triad, which specializes in recycling textiles, about 900,000 tons of clothing and shoes are thrown away in the UK every year. We are buying so much that 75 per cent of it ends up in landfill after we have owned it for less than 6 months. Even the charity shops are at full capacity and are often unable to accept the clothes we have bought on a cheap whim and not because we needed them.

Consider where and how clothes have been made. It is becoming easier to source organic or at least fair trade fabrics, and designers are more aware that the provenance of their garments is as important as their appearance. We will always be influenced by the price of new clothes, but it is more important to be aware of their value – not because of a designer label, but because of how the garment has been made and what it has been made from. Probably the best advice I can offer is to be aware of what you are buying:

- Be aware of social justice.
- Buy good-quality clothing for a fair price.
- Buy one good piece for every 10 cheap pieces you might have bought in the past, and look after it.

As part of this new regime spend time on finding clothes that will last, that are of good quality and cut, and that will suit your lifestyle. Turn your back on fashion fads – by which I mean anything that will embarrass you or your children in two years' time. A good starting point is to sort out your existing wardrobe.

Matching hangers

Begin with matching hangers. A well-organized, presentable wardrobe will make life a million times easier and it will be a pleasure to choose from. During the early days at Cabbages & Roses we acquired wire hangers from our local dry cleaners at no cost, and spent many a happy hour binding them with the white waste selvedges of our fabrics. Ranks of white bound hangers made a very pleasing display – it was an extremely cheap and useful reclamation exercise. The clothes never slipped off the dry cotton, which transformed harsh wire into a chic display at no cost. If you haven't the time or inclination to sit covering wire hangers for hours (even bearing in mind the therapeutic benefits of the task), just make sure all the hangers in your wardrobe are the same – this is important for a calm, coordinated, easy-to-choose-from display, something you will be grateful for when getting dressed in a hurry.

BELOW: *Matching clothes hangers make for an orderly wardrobe.*

patching clothes

When a hole or tear appears in a favourite item of clothing, try patching it. The patch should be of the same, or similar, material to the main garment, but as for colour and pattern – that all depends on what you can lay your hands on and your imagination. So long as they are complementary rather than clashing, choose whatever fabric you like.

you will need

Fabric of suitable colour and pattern
Needle and thread to match fabric
Scissors
Pins

1 Measure the tear in the garment and cut out a square or rectangular piece of fabric that allows enough to cover it plus a surplus of 5cm (2in) on each side.

2 On the wrong side, turn over about 1cm (½in) on each side and sew, neatly folding in the corners.

3 Then turn over 1cm (½in) and sew, again neatly folding in the corners. The cut edges of the patch are then turned in, which prevents fraying.

4 Position the patch on the garment, secure with pins and then stitch neatly in place.

Sorting your clothes

Rearrange your clothes. If you haven't worn something for two years, get rid of it. In my experience it is a huge muddle of too many clothes that leads a woman's brain to believe that she has nothing to wear and to get overwhelmed by the urge to buy more, only adding to the muddle. Certainly, I could manage with 10 pieces of clothing. I shall 'cull and consolidate' and urge you to do the same.

It is far better to have a few perfect items than to have hundreds of cheap ones. Just like growing your own food, having less makes one appreciate what one does have. Presuming that you will be left only with things that you love, it will be much easier to spend time repairing, reviving and perhaps re-modelling them.

This is also a very good reason/excuse to go and buy proper clothes from proper shops. Choose beautiful garments that will fill you with glee for at least the next five years. If five T-shirts can be bought for £5.00, $5.00 or 5 euros, you can bet your bottom dollar (£, euro) that someone, somewhere is NOT benefiting.

Recycling clothes

In the enormous sort-out that you are about to do/have done, reuse and recycle as much as you can. Old T-shirts can be cut up and used as dusters, and tights can be cut up and used as bags to fill with lavender. Tights also make a very good plant tie, so keep a stock of them in the garden shed.

Recycle by organizing a clothes swap with your friends – one woman's big mistake is another woman's heavenly new dress/coat/skirt. If you have exhausted all avenues of disposal (charity shops, friends, children), take your old clothes to a recycling centre.

Mending

If a button on a garment is missing, and you cannot find an identical replacement, consider changing all the buttons for mis-matched, coloured ones. If a hole or permanent stain appears due to moth damage or an accident, try repairing or patching it. Some dry cleaners offer an invisible mending service if you feel you are not up to repairing it yourself. Classic, good-quality clothes are worth preserving; fashion fads that might look ridiculous in a few years' time are probably not!

Storing

Before storing clothes, it is vital to make sure they are clean. If moths afflict your home – and they are a growing problem with the current fashion for buying second-hand or vintage clothing – dry cleaning is an effective although not environmentally kind solution. It will, however, kill the larvae that do the damage to clothes. The female moth lays her eggs on natural fabrics – cottons, wool and silks. Moths are less keen on man-made fibres. If the garment is clean but you want to make sure that it will not become a larvae feast in storage, put it into the freezer for a couple of days sealed in a plastic or waxed paper bag – this not only kills moths but also their eggs.

Moth larvae enjoy human 'soil' so it is essential that you store clean clothes only. Never store dry-cleaned clothes in the dry cleaner's plastic covering as the residue of the chemicals in an airless space can turn the clothes inside yellow. There are many natural moth deterrents – the best are lavender, lemon peel, bay leaves, cinnamon, rosemary and cedar wood. All of these will lose their efficacy after about a year, so must be replaced regularly. Clean the inside of the wardrobe regularly and carefully. Vacuum the hidden dark corners where moth larvae might be lurking.

Lavender bags

These are wonderful gifts, especially because they need refreshing regularly. Cut out large quantities of muslin squares, fill with dried lavender and tie the tops with ribbon. Put them in pockets of clothing both in the wardrobe and in storage to deter moths from setting up home.

Air and admire your clothes

If you have the inclination and a sturdy washing line in your garden, hang your clothes out to air on very cold, bright and frosty days, turn out the pockets and brush each garment with a sturdy brush to get rid of any larvae or their parents. Moths dislike the cold and dislike bright light even more. Not only does this practice deter moths but a jolly good brush and shake in the dry, cold air will make all your clothes look and smell as if they have been freshly cleaned.

LEFT: *Since babies grow so quickly and their sweet tiny socks have a very short useful life, reuse these little treasures by turning them into lavender bags.*

RIGHT: *Keep old cotton frocks and skirts beyond their useful life for transforming into patches, dusters or smaller items of clothing.*

Caring for shoes

There are a few simple guidelines for looking after your shoes and boots so that they last you for years.

▶ Keep them clean and polished.
▶ Repair the soles and heels of shoes and boots as soon as possible to avoid permanent damage.
▶ Fill wet shoes and boots tightly with crumpled newspaper to keep them in shape and leave them to dry naturally, then feed them with a really good natural polish.
▶ To remove odours from shoes, sprinkle bicarbonate of soda inside them and leave for a couple of hours.
▶ Plimsoles, my preferred choice of shoe for the entire summer, can be washed in the washing machine. Buy two or three pairs so that they never need to be worn more than once before washing.

BELOW: *Like fine wine, classic washable plimsoles improve with age!*

Laundering clothes

Wash cotton and other machine-washable clothes at low temperatures – 30 degrees is perfectly adequate – with a cup full of bicarbonate of soda (see page 30) added to the soap powder. This makes washing powder much more effective and helps to extend the life of your washing machine. Add a cup of white distilled vinegar (see page 22) to the dispenser drawer instead of fabric conditioner to remove chemical residues and soften the fibres of the clothes.

When buying a new washing machine, check its green credentials and opt for the greenest appliance possible – they are not necessarily more expensive. If you have the option of an eco-wash in the programme, it will go some way to relieve your guilt when you follow my next instruction.

To keep beautiful, new, white underwear white, avoid washing it in too full a load. It is over-filling your machine that causes white underwear to turn grey. If your underwear is particularly precious, wash it by hand.

To treat stains, soak the item as soon as possible – fresh stains are much easier to deal with than dried stains – in a basin filled with a solution of bicarbonate of soda and warm water. In an emergency, lemon juice is also a good stain remover as it has bleaching properties. Rub half a lemon onto the stain, squeezing some of the juice directly onto it, then rinse with warm water. Never use hot water as this can set the stain rather than remove it.

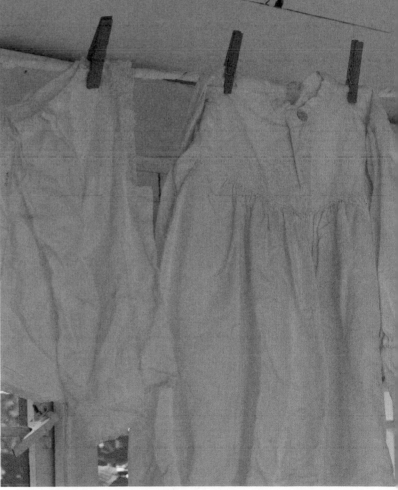

RIGHT: *To keep your whites white, simply avoid over-loading the machine, rather than adding chemical whiteners to the wash.*

BELOW: *Soak stained fabric in bicarbonate of soda to remove the blemish.*

Good drying practices

Dry clothes, if possible, outside in the fresh air. When the weather is inclement, air them inside on a wooden rack. This is always preferable to tumble drying, not only because it lessens carbon emissions but because your clothes will last longer if you avoid tumble drying them.

A charming drying practice from long ago is to spread small items – pillowcases, underwear, baby's clothes and socks – on lavender bushes in the warm sun. The fibres will absorb the scent of lavender. This method is especially lovely for night gowns and pillowcases – both adults' and children's – as the essential oil in lavender is known to promote restful sleep.

SMALL THINGS THAT CAN MAKE A BIG DIFFERENCE

- Investigate 'wet clean' laundries to deal with your 'dry clean only' items of clothing. They use a combination of steam, pure soap and vacuuming to clean 'dry clean only' clothes.
- Hand washing is always an eco-friendly option for dealing with small amounts of laundry.
- Instead of using bleach to whiten small cotton items, boil for a few minutes in a solution of water and lemon juice.
- Heating the water accounts for 90 per cent of the energy used in washing machines – 30 degrees is ample.
- Instead of using fabric softeners in your washing machine, which can leave chemical residue on your clothes, use white distilled vinegar to soften fabrics.
- If you want scented clothes and laundry, store lavender and herb bags, soap and essential oils in the laundry cupboard. The linens will absorb the fragrances into their fibres.
- Use powdered or tablet washing products in the washing machine and dishwasher. Liquid versions contain twice as many harmful chemicals.

LEFT: *Avoid using a tumble dryer as much as possible, not only to reduce carbon emissions but also to make your fabrics last longer.*

RIGHT: *A plentiful supply of wooden clothes pegs and a sturdy length of washing line can save countless units of electricity, with the added bonus that clothes dried in the open air always seem to smell fresher.*

The linen cupboard

Just like the wardrobe, a good clear out and tidy up of the linen cupboard does so much for morale, not to mention efficiency. As obvious as it may seem, divide the linen cupboard into well-labelled sections – it is something that will save so much time and encourage those with access to the cupboard to keep it as tidy as they found it.

To distinguish between single, double, queen-size and king-size bed linen, create a colour-coded labelling system using coloured ribbon, braid or tape sewn onto each corner of the linen. A single corner is never enough because that will be the one neatly folded and hidden within the pile, and trying to get to it will cause chaos in the cupboard.

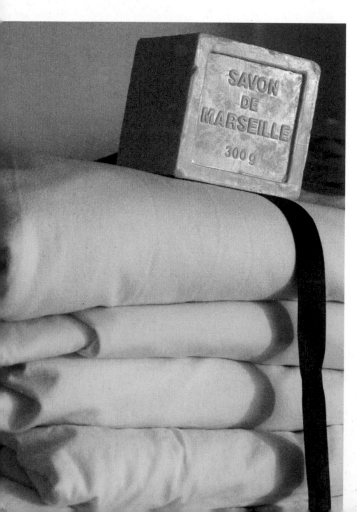

If you have inherited beautiful linens but find they are never used, tie them up in a pile with ribbon. This neat, orderly and beautiful pile of linen will enhance the shelves and even if the rest of the cupboard falls into disarray, the beribboned pile will remain stately and give the appearance of a well-ordered household.

To keep the cupboard smelling sweet and free from moths (although these should not be a problem if the linens are regularly washed and hung out to air), slip lavender bags into the piles.

LEFT: *Store scented soap in the linen cupboard so that stacks of neatly folded sheets absorb a gentle aroma.*

RIGHT: *An orderly linen cupboard will bring much pleasure.*

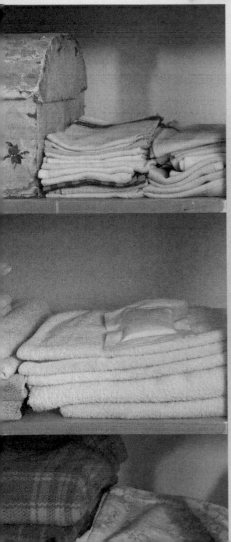

CHAPTER 2

ENERGY FOR LIFE

In Europe and the USA we still enjoy low-cost energy and an abundance of water compared with many parts of the world, and as a result we tend to squander these vital resources. We have huge reserves of cheap energy from prehistoric times, with vast areas of forest covering the land and enormous reserves of coal, and our own North Sea oil and gas, but all these gifts are finite and all will, eventually, run out.

We depend (and I am not saying this is a bad thing) on other countries to provide much of our fuel. The bad part about this dependence is the possibility that one day we may find ourselves without the fuel to warm ourselves, to transport food and to run our factories. A solution to this and other impending self-inflicted problems is to look back at the lives of our forefathers who worked with nature and the natural world and had the expertise to be self-sufficient.

Water

While we have a climate in the United Kingdom that has given us abundant rainfall, and summer droughts have been an infrequent event (1976 and 2006 being the last two of note), there is no doubt that the weather is changing and we seem to be moving towards feast or famine with regard to water. Almost tropical downpours in July 2007 caused huge flood damage to many parts of the world, exacerbated by the madness of building houses on flood plains and the lack of thought regarding surface water drainage from built-up areas, bringing home to us the fact that we are not well prepared for extreme weather.

Warnings are now being voiced that the zeitgeist of replacing grass lawns with wooden decking and paved areas is another cause of flooding. Rainfall can seep into a lawn but remains on the surface of ground that is inappropriately clad.

BELOW: *Water is a precious resource upon which life depends. It should be treated with respect.*

The cost of fuel

Without doubt, energy costs will – and should – rise. The cost of energy has to reflect not just the supply and demand issue but also the environmental damage caused by different fuel sources. We are all in the same boat because, whichever country energy sources are derived from, environmental damage will be the same.

Energy is a resource imported and exported throughout the world – often from areas of political instability – and with no guarantee that it will continue to be available at a price we can afford, at a time when we need it, from a country that is willing to sell it to us. Emerging economies are energy hungry and world reserves of hydrocarbon fuels are finite, with refining and distribution capacity struggling to meet demand – a demand that can only get worse. The question we should ask ourselves is why are we burning unrenewable fuels when we know the damage they do to the environment and when their sustainability is in doubt.

BELOW: *A well-kept woodland can produce power to heat homes in a sustainable way.*

Reducing energy in the home

The first thing for us to do is to reduce the energy used in the home. As individuals, there are a number of steps we can take, which need not impact too dramatically on our comfort or ability to lead a satisfactory lifestyle.

Lifestyle changes

▌ Rise with the lark to make best use of the natural daylight.

▌ Travel by rail instead of by air, if necessary reworking your schedule to give yourself more time.

▌ Clean the windows and get used to using natural light instead of electric light.

▌ Wear more clothes when it is cold rather than switching on the heating.

▌ If you live in a hot climate, limit your use of air conditioning by planting shade-giving trees in appropriate positions to minimize strong sun getting into the house.

▌ In a hot climate, make a through draught by opening windows and doors that are opposite each other. You might consider making new window openings (it might be necessary to obtain planning permission).

▌ If you live in a cold climate, properly insulated wooden floors absorb heat and keep it for longer. Make sure the boards are laid without gaps that will cause draughts.

▌ Get your house inspected by a qualified insulation advisor. You will receive advice on all aspects of energy saving, not to mention money saving.

▌ Interline curtains for extra draught-proofing. Sew old blankets between curtain fabric and lining.

▌ Place a brick or filled litre bottle of water inside the lavatory cistern. This will save at least one litre (1¾ pints) of water every time you flush.

▌ Brush your teeth with the water tap turned off. Only turn on as necessary.

Household appliances

▌ Only buy appliances certified as energy efficient.

▌ There is no need to rinse dishes before putting them into the dishwasher – scrape remains into the dustbin instead.

▌ Run the dishwasher or washing machine with full loads, as much as possible.

▌ Keep appliances running efficiently so that they use less electricity. Keep the heat exchanger at the back of the refrigerator dust

LEFT: *Boots made for walking – the very best form of green transport!*

free, and clean the inside of the dishwasher and washing machine with a solution of white distilled vinegar and bicarbonate of soda.

- Defrost your freezer regularly.
- Avoid empty spaces in the freezer. Fill the empty parts of the freezer with bags of ice.
- Empty the fridge if you are going away for a week or more. Switch it off and leave the door open – there is little point in keeping it running if it is empty.
- Switch off unnecessary lights and use localized lamps instead of overhead lighting.
- Use low-energy light bulbs. By changing all your normal light bulbs to compact fluorescent bulbs, you could save 75 per cent of the energy you would have used.
- Install a timer on light switches so that, when you are away, you don't need to leave lights on to deter burglars.
- Unplug chargers as soon as they have done their job. Up to 95 per cent of energy used by chargers is wasted.
- Switch off appliances when not in use. It is not necessary to have the television, CD and DVD players on stand-by. Dishwashers and washing machines should also be switched off at the wall sockets when not in use.

Kitchen practices

- Boil only as much water as you need.
- When cooking with boiling water, boil it in the kettle rather than on the stove. This saves half the amount of energy required.
- Chop vegetables smaller so that they cook quicker, using less power.
- Make use of a slate cold shelf in the larder, if you have one, for those items of food that do not need refrigeration. Never put hot food in the fridge. Instead, leave in the larder until cool enough to refrigerate.

RIGHT: *An alternative form of transport, with no impact on the environment and a beneficial impact on your health.*

Reducing our carbon footprint

According to online encyclopedia Wikipedia, there are 6.6 billion people in this world. If we presume that just one third of those people live in houses and all that one third of the population made these small changes to their lives, imagine how much energy those 2.2 billion people could save.

The greatest energy consumption per head is in our home and in our travel. Both these areas are within our control to moderate, and it need not cost us anything. Indeed it will save us all a great deal of money. By insulating our homes and using central heating only when absolutely necessary, by investing in heat recovery systems and installing intelligent control systems and more efficient boilers, we can do a huge amount to reduce our carbon footprint. Initially, these measures will cost money, but in the long run they will be less expensive than excessive oil or gas consumption, both to our pockets and, more importantly, to the environment.

RIGHT: *Avoid using chemical firelighters. A store of pine cones, dried lemon shells, twigs and tightly rolled newspaper is all you need to start a fire.*

BELOW: *Neatly stacked wood for fuel.*

Alternative energy sources

Once we have reduced our energy demand, we need to look at how to generate our reduced energy needs from fuels and sources that do not damage the environment. These should be sustainable and available – locally, where possible, to give us the security of supply.

In Europe, the energy used in homes produces more climate-changing greenhouse gases than the continent's entire manufacturing industry.

For many, especially those who live in urban areas, the options for alternative fuels and energy sources for homes are more limited than for those who live in semi-rural and rural areas, purely because of space. However, there are systems tailor-made for individual properties and community schemes that are kind to the environment. Check the websites of energy providers to discover whether you are in a position to receive a greener power.

There are free sources of energy – as ever, kindly supplied by Mother Nature – but the harvesting of such energy often comes at a cost, both in monetary terms and environmental impact.

Wind farms and wind turbines

The capital cost of setting up wind farms is huge because the infrastructure required to connect them to the electric grid is costly. Some people also regard them as visually intrusive – personally, I find them exciting and beautiful. However, they only work when the wind blows so we cannot depend on them entirely. Wind farms need the back-up of coal, gas or oil, called a 'turning reserve'.

However, Britain is the windiest country in Europe with enough offshore wind to power the country three times over. According to Good Energy,

Britian's only 100 per cent renewable electricity supplier, we have the potential to power ourselves cleanly without relying on gas pipelines from other countries. If we start now, we could make the transition over the next 40–50 years. In the meantime, those that we have make a contribution and, in my opinion, are a worthwhile investment.

For individuals, the options are to buy energy from a 'green' supplier, or, subject to planning regulations, to install your own wind turbine (and solar panels – see right). Anything less than 6kW is probably only snipping at the edges of being economic. However, if you live in a very windy part of the world, electricity providers will buy your wind power if you have a surplus.

LEFT: *If you burn wood, save the ash to use in the garden. Sprinkle it around plants to deter slugs from eating new shoots.*

Tidal power and hydropower

Although probably not a very convenient solution for most individuals, tidal power is another option. The tide is guaranteed and the power systems using tidal power are known to work. However, the capital costs are enormous.

Hydropower has proved itself to be efficient, albeit with huge installation costs, and requires ugly pylons and cables. While the infrastructure could be buried underground, environmental damage might outweigh the benefits. However, it is another option for the experts to work on. Individual homes or communities can benefit from hydropower if there is access to a water resource of sufficient volume and flow. The installation of turbines in existing mills is a very real prospect as the major engineering work has already been done. Smaller schemes relying on the head of water rather than the volume can take advantage of small, efficient generating plants.

Solar power

This power works well when the sun shines. Either direct solar heat or photo-voltaic cells generate electricity. The technology is getting better and less costly, and can work well for individual houses. Local government can help by making planning permission less restrictive on the installation of solar panels, and designers can help by improving their appearance. As part of a multi-technology installation, solar power can contribute to year-round energy.

Biofuels

These fuels are produced from material that has been grown specifically for fuel production, or from material grown for other purposes that has generated a by-product once called 'waste'. A recent criticism of the policy of taking vast acreages out of food production and diverting the crops to bio-ethanol and bio-diesel production was that it potentially creates a shortage in world food supply.

This is a knee-jerk, selfish and not very efficient policy to create road fuel. Worse still is the ripping up of rainforest to accommodate palm oil plantations. Both these practices are counter-productive and ecologically disastrous. As long as people are a priority in the agenda of those providing road fuel, then the above solutions can be of real benefit, but when money is at the forefront of this progress, it is inevitable that the poor will suffer short term, and the rich in the long term.

RIGHT: *Electric lighting within the garden will increase your carbon footprint. Candles in jam jars are far more beautiful than even the cleverest outdoor lighting scheme.*

The future of energy supply

We can all help simply by reducing our dependence on cars. Governments can help by making public transport more user friendly, cheaper and more efficient.

There is scope for growing specific crops for energy, but only where there is no conflict with food production and environmental issues. Miscanthus (elephant grass) and short-rotation coppice, such as willow and poplar, are two good examples of this.

In the first instance we need to focus on converting existing agricultural and forestry by-products and waste to a fuel source that can be utilized to produce heat and, to a lesser extent, power. This can range from wood chip through to straw and cereal wastes and processed wood waste. There is also the option of converting animal and human waste to generate electricity and heat.

Incineration of domestic and industrial waste – subject to careful control of incineration flue gases – is also a viable concept at an industrial scale as well as on a smaller scale.

LEFT AND RIGHT: *A sustainable source of heating fuel.*

Forestry benefits

Increasing the area of land under forestry to produce sustainable wood for fuel would provide an endless resource. Planting and managing woodland also reduces carbon emissions because of the CO_2 absorbed and the oxygen given out by growing trees, and land is stabilized by the growing roots of trees.

More immediately, there is in tiny England in excess of 60,000 hectares (148,000 acres) of unmanaged woodland. If this huge acreage was managed carefully, it could produce wood fuel on a sustainable rotational basis. This would vastly improve the biodiversity of woodland, create employment in rural areas and provide a source of income for woodland owners. Five million tonnes of wood waste is committed to landfill every year in the UK alone. This equates to 1,059,322 tonnes of oil. Oil produces 3.127 tonnes of CO_2 per tonne, which equates to 331,250 tonnes of CO_2. If we burnt all this waste wood efficiently, the CO_2 emissions fall to 31,250 tonnes, a reduction of some 300,000 tonnes for the same amount of heat produced. If you read this paragraph again, and then again, you will see how significant that saving would be.

If transport and landfill tax are taken into account, the cost to industry of dumping five million tonnes of wood waste to landfill is £4.24 billion a year, of which the government collect £1.05 billion in landfill tax. It is, therefore, not surprising that governments are not quite as keen as they might be to prevent the dumping of wood waste.

Nuclear fuel is an option but, just as we thought it a good idea to mince up cow carcases and feed them to their offspring, my opinion is that, until we know how to clean up the potential mess, we should not proceed – there are other solutions.

CHAPTER 3

THE KITCHEN GARDEN

Growing your own fruit and vegetables has major
health benefits. Firstly, it forces you to take exercise in
the fresh air. The exertion needed for proper digging is
as close to aerobic exercise as I shall ever get, plus we
live in an area of extreme hills, so wheeling a barrow
full of waste must be equivalent to at least an hour
of walking on a treadmill.

Secondly, you benefit from knowing exactly
what your crops have been sprayed and fed with.
Another health benefit is the speedy transference
from the earth to your plate, which means that fruit
and vegetables retain more essential vitamins and
minerals. Eaten moments after picking, they taste so
much better than those transported halfway across the
world. Over time, sugars convert into starch and, the
longer the journey, the less sugar and more starch
food contains. The difference in the taste of home-
grown or locally grown fruit and vegetables is like
the difference between a tinned peach and one
freshly plucked from a tree.

Compost

Entire books have been written on the subject of composting, but as far as I am concerned, there are three reasons to compost. Firstly, because I am just a bit squeamish about slugs and other wildlife setting up home in fruit, putting suspect items into the compost bin slightly mitigates the wasteful nature of my fastidious eating habits. Knowing that they will rot to become a beautiful, black, loamy substance that will improve the soil and encourage new growth in the garden placates my conscience. Secondly, composting eases the load of waste collectors and therefore the quantity of landfill waste, and thus the release of carbon emissions from slowly rotting food. The third reason is the magical way that waste products become a valuable source of nutrients and soil improvers to the soil, giving back what has been taken from the earth.

'The soil is the gift of God to the Living'

Thomas Jefferson, 1813

BENEFITS OF COMPOSTING

▶ Compost enriches the soil by increasing the organic matter so that plants are healthier and stronger.
▶ It provides natural, slow-release nutrients.
▶ Not only does compost help the soil to retain moisture but it also balances the pH levels.
▶ Compost reduces soil erosion.
▶ In winter, compost increases soil temperature, while in summer it lowers it, thus benefiting the plants.
▶ Sandy soils improve by gaining body, which will preserve moisture. Clay soils will gain a more open structure so they drain better.

And all of this comes from what we consider to be waste material and would otherwise find itself in landfill. Good enough reasons, surely, for all of us with a garden, however large or small, to start composting with a vengeance.

Kitchen compost bins

My kitchen compost bin is a vintage white enamel bucket. Probably 80 years old, it is still going strong. It is easy to clean and has a wholesome, traditional look about it.

I never cover my compost bucket while it is in the kitchen. The main reason is so that it does not get forgotten and begin its festering process inside the house. During the summer months you will need to empty the kitchen compost bin daily as it tends to attract flies; in winter this is less of a problem.

LEFT: *My kitchen compost bin, recycling vegetable matter into wholesome compost for the garden.*

What to compost

Any raw vegetable matter that will rot down quickly is suitable for a compost heap. While decomposing, the compost heap will heat up and the weeds should rot. However, it is a wise precaution never to put infected or diseased plants or weeds in seed into the compost heap. Put them on the bonfire instead to make sure that the viruses are completely destroyed.

I incorporate flower water and the dregs from coffeepot and teapot for their moisture content. As with all house and garden matters, trial and error is key – what works for some might not work for others. However, a good result is unmistakable – a dark, black soil with no hint as to what it has been made from. The following will all make good compost:

- Vegetable peelings
- Vegetables and fruits way beyond their sell-by date
- Dead flowers, along with the old flower water
- Fallen petals and leaves
- Corrugated cardboard
- Egg boxes
- Coffee grounds
- Tea leaves and teabags
- Egg shells (never whole eggs)
- Grass cuttings
- Weeds (not in seed and never bindweed)
- Torn-up newspaper
- Straw (essential)
- Fruit peelings – there is a debate about citrus fruit but I put it in with no detrimental effect. (If you worry about putting citrus peelings into the compost heap, save lemon and orange shells, leave them to dry and use them as firelighters – see page 64.)

Never put cooked food (even vegetable waste) into the compost bin as this attracts vermin.

Types of compost bin

Although I have survived with a single wooden bin that is built to resemble a bee hive, in an ideal world you would make three compartments for your vegetable compost. One is for newly added waste, the second for shovelling the contents of the first compartment into, adding air and straw as you go in the turning process, and the third for storing the mature compost. If you have access to animal manure, the compost bin only needs two separate compartments. In one, turn the compost and allow it to mature; in the other, store the finished, mature compost before use.

Keep bins with processing compost covered to prevent saturation by the rain and to keep in heat, which speeds up the rotting process. A piece of coir matting or old (not rubber-backed) wool carpet is suitable for this task.

Site the compost bins, which should ideally measure 1.2 metres (4 feet) square, in an area that is easy to access with a wheelbarrow, in a site where there is good air circulation but out of the wind, and away from fierce sun.

'40% of household waste can be composted at home, saving 20% of the UK's methane emissions from the slow decomposition of biodegradable landfill waste.'

The Composting Association

ABOVE: *Egg boxes can be added to the compost heap, or used as containers for planting seeds.*

making compost

The main thing you need to make compost is patience as it can take a long time for your household and garden waste to rot down into lovely, rich, crumbly earth. You can use a plastic urban bin, a two- or three-compartment wooden one, or just allocate a place in the garden to build a heap with no bin at all. Whatever you decide, air, moisture and nitrogen are all essential ingredients for making good compost.

you will need

Plastic or wooden bin (optional)
Straw
Garden waste
Household waste
Water
Activator
Garden fork

1 Stand the bin or build the heap on earth (not concrete or paving) so that worms can get in easily, and put down a layer of straw or twigs to allow air to circulate.

2 Add a layer of grass cuttings and weeds, and if they are dry, sprinkle with water.

3 Then add the contents of your kitchen compost bucket and keep adding suitable material, plus water when the heap gets too dry. Untreated cardboard tubes, such as empty kitchen rolls, help to add air.

4 Every week or so, turn the heap with a garden fork and make sure the nitrogen content is boosted with activators to speed up the rotting process. Good natural activators include comfrey leaves, grass cuttings, urine and animal manure if you have access to it (but not from cats or dogs). Otherwise, commercial activators are available.

Council composting schemes

Some councils have composting schemes whereby vegetable matter is delivered to a central store and compost is made from 'donated' garden waste. However well meaning these schemes are, be aware that, unknowingly, some infected plants or annoyingly persistent weeds might lurk therein. Unless you are prepared to keep the compost for at least two years without using it, do not apply it to your garden. Many years of hard work could be ruined by the introduction of bindweed or potato blight. The best compost is your own compost as you know exactly what it has been made from.

Poultry and farmyard manure

You can add fresh chicken, horse and cow manure to the compost heap in small amounts, or apply well-rotted farmyard manure directly onto the ground. The solid part of the manure is rich in phosphates, while the urine contains nitrogen and potash, all of which are vital ingredients for healthy plant growth.

    If you do add fresh chicken manure, make sure that the chickens have been reared organically. Poultry manure is richer than farmyard manure – six times richer in nitrogen and four times richer in phosphorus and

BELOW: *Manure acquired from happy, healthy chickens makes an excellent addition to the compost heap.*

potassium. Fresh chicken waste acts as an accelerator, speeding up the heating process within the vegetable compost heap. Organic chicken manure pellets can also be spread directly onto the ground – follow the instructions on the packet.

Urban gardeners can buy organic manures – the internet is a mine of information for supplies of organic gardening requisites. Investigate the source of the compost, if possible visiting the supplier. It is not unknown for some unscrupulous traders to claim their product is organic in order to charge much higher prices, when actually it is anything but.

Animal manure alone is an excellent fertilizer and soil improver but should be well rotted before use. However, you cannot always be sure as to the age of the manure even if you are acquiring it from a local stable or farm. To avoid infecting your garden with weed seeds that have not completely rotted, I suggest you store the manure for at least a year or, better still, two years before use.

In the third century, the Romans encouraged their farm labourers to urinate into the compost heap. Today organic soil experts tell us that urine is still the best nitrogenous activator nature and man can supply. I leave it to you to decide whether or how it should be added.

Spent mushroom compost

This improves the soil. Laid in a thick layer, it prevents weeds from growing and conserves heat and moisture. Suppliers can be found on the internet.

Bracken and lambswool compost

Simon Bland and Jane Barker, hill farmers in the Lake District, have created a compost using bracken and lambswool. Bracken is very high in nutrients, while wool has good water retention and is an excellent source of nitrogen. The recipe took six years to perfect, and it produces a soft, peat-like compost. However, unlike peat, the compost is made from waste products and does not have any damaging impact on the environment. For further information, visit their website: www.dalefootcomposts.co.uk.

ABOVE RIGHT: *Mushroom compost conserves both heat and moisture, and is an excellent soil improver.*

RIGHT: *Organically reared sheep provide wool which, when added to compost, makes it rich in nitrogen.*

Allotments

If you don't have a large garden, investigate renting an allotment. Although you can use a courtyard, balcony or roof terrace to grow at least some fresh fruit and vegetables – in pots, growbags, bins, old baths and china sinks, indeed anything that can hold earth and water – an allotment gives you more opportunity for diversity.

How allotments work

Allotments have been an important and valuable part of urban communities for over 150 years. They were created to empower those on low incomes to improve the quality of their lives, their health and their diet by growing their own food.

Allotments proved invaluable during the Second World War and interest peaked as people responded to Britain's 'Dig for Victory' demand for self-sufficiency. All town gardens, including the gardens at Buckingham Palace, were turned into miniature farms. One and a half million plots on allotments were cultivated and during this period 1.3 million tons of food were grown on 1.4 million plots every year. That is nearly one ton of food from each plot.

Today, allotments are increasingly valued for their therapeutic benefits, providing a quiet refuge where people have the sense of gardening in the country – a wholesome social community within an urban environment. This, along with our concerns over food safety, air miles travelled by our food, and the desire to reduce our carbon footprint, has made allotment gardening altogether a rather fashionable pursuit.

There are 330,000 allotments in the United Kingdom, which can cost as little as £25 a year to rent. The increased interest in growing organic vegetables and fruit untainted with chemicals and pesticides, and in eating food that has not been genetically modified or irradiated, has resulted in long waiting lists for allotments. Happily, the councils who are responsible for their administration are keen to oblige. They keep a close eye on how the parcels of land are run. Strict adherence to the rules results in a good turnover of those tenants who do not appreciate or are unable to care for their allocated plot.

Most allotments are charming, and some are very beautiful. The gardeners are willing to share advice and experience, making for a huge diversity of knowledge and plant life. Some allotments are equipped with sheds,

RIGHT: *Apples grown on a cordon take up little space on an allotment.*

greenhouses and chicken coops, and all have an atmosphere harking back to the 1950s, even though high-speed trains and low-flying aircraft interrupt garden chat and cups of tea made on ancient gas burners and drunk from old enamel cups.

A need for healthier lifestyles

In Europe and the USA we are increasingly affluent but, in spite of this, the original need for allotments as a means of improving the quality of life for those on low incomes remains. Startlingly, studies have revealed that under-nutrition still remains a problem within our cities, even though obesity is prevalent and a major concern in poorer communities.

This anxiety over our diet is acknowledged at government level with increasing concern regarding obesity in the population. Public health campaigns are consistently emphasizing the importance of a diet high in fruit and vegetables, along with adequate exercise.

'Nearly two thirds of men and over half of women in England are now overweight or obese. And the problem here is increasing faster than in most other European countries. If prevalence continues to rise at the current rate, more than one in four adults will be obese by 2010. This would significantly increase the incidence of associated diseases, such as coronary heart disease, and would cost the economy over £3.5 billion a year by that date.'

Sir John Bourne
Head of the National
Audit Office, *'Tackling Obesity in England'*
February 2004

FAR LEFT (CLOCKWISE): *Bolted lettuces can be used to make good compost; a black sunflower grown to attract birds and bees (the seeds are both edible and easy to collect for next year's crop); strong and healthy rhubarb stems; strawberries growing in an old tin bath.*

LEFT: *Essential allotment supplies – a gas burner for brewing tea, plus vintage enamel mugs.*

the kitchen garden **81**

Green gardening

Although I cannot claim to know all that much about gardening, I have, after a fashion, managed to keep our small plot happy and healthy for the past 27 years. Trial and error is my method, backed up by tips and advice from proper gardeners – there is always something more to learn. We are self-sufficient (mostly) for at least three months of the year. When time allows I will store crops efficiently and be more adventurous in my planting, and one day I shall have a greenhouse (the glass sort) where I can take cuttings, raise seeds and be self-sufficient for at least six months of the year.

A basic guide to propagating

Most plants will grow from seed, especially in the vegetable garden. However, larger plants can be propagated by division or by cuttings. Layering, root cuttings and grafting can also increase your plant inventory, but these three tasks require more knowledge than I have to explain clearly. They are quite complicated and not guaranteed to work. If you really want to know how to perform them, buy a book dedicated to the subject.

However, growing plants from seed is magical, growing from cuttings is fulfilling and dividing established plants is hard work but nonetheless extremely gratifying.

Growing from seed

Growing from seed is the simplest and least expensive method of raising large numbers of plants.

The best time to sow seeds is in spring, with some sown in autumn, although successional planting throughout the seasons ensures a supply for longer. There are suggestions for dealing with the glut you will inevitably find yourself with in Chapter 4, The Well-stocked Larder (see pages 122–144). All you need to know will be on the seed packet, unless you have been given seeds by a grower, in which case ask them for the sowing instructions. As a general rule of thumb, seeds should be sown at a depth equal to their thickness. I have yet to learn to pay proper attention to instructions and, more often than not, plant seeds too far apart or too close together. I am always surprised that plants really do grow from 20cm (8in) to 2m (8 feet) within a growing season – so believe what you read!

Start tender plants that will be affected by frost indoors, in a greenhouse or cold frame, from February to March. From March to April sow hardy annuals directly into the ground where you want them to grow and flower.

Herbaceous plants can be sown indoors in February or March or outdoors in late April or May. Once you have made your planting plan and bought your seeds, there is nothing standing in your way to start growing all your own flowers and vegetables for the whole season ahead and, if stored carefully, into the winter too.

BELOW: *Hand-thrown flowerpots – more ecologically sound than their plastic equivalents.*

Materials and equipment

Without going into complicated detail – and it is not complicated – you will need the following for growing your own crops from seed:

1 Seed compost Make sure it is organic. Never buy peat as this is an unsustainable product which, even though organic, is not ecologically friendly. Seed compost is a combination of sterilized loam, sand and chalk. It is simpler to buy seed compost – home-made versions are difficult to sterilize and the necessary ingredients are not easy to source.

2 Seed tray or small pots An egg tray is a very eco-friendly container for small seedlings, allowing them to be planted directly into the soil in their biodegradable pots without disturbing the tiny root systems. Similarly, you can make your own pots with newspaper (see page 86).

If you are re-using an old seed tray or pot, make sure it is clean and does not carry old viruses or moulds from previous planting or old age. To disinfect it, wash with a solution of one part warm water and one part distilled white vinegar.

3 Watering can with rose head

LEFT: *Seedlings started in empty cardboard egg boxes can be planted straight into the ground without disturbing the fragile roots.*

Planting seeds

Fill the container with compost, lightly firming with your hand, or shake gently to distribute the soil evenly. Following directions on the seed packet, either sow larger seeds in rows or scatter finer seeds on the surface of the soil. Cover with a thin layer of compost. When sowing fine seeds it is sometimes easier to control where they fall, and to distribute them more evenly, if you mix them with a small amount of sand before sowing.

ABOVE: *Young seedlings, planted in plugs.*

LEFT: *Pots placed on top of sticks protect gardeners from wounding themselves on the sticks and also confuse birds and other creatures, thus protecting the emerging pea crop.*

newspaper plant pots

For providing a feelgood factor, these planters are ideal. They are not difficult to make, are excellent for raising your own plants from seed – and they take all the effort out of the job of planting out. If you don't have a suitable jar to hand, you can use a rolling pin.

you will need

Newspaper

Scissors

Straight jar or rolling pin

Damp compost

Seeds

Wooden seed tray or plate

1 Cut or tear newspaper into pieces measuring 20 x 12.5cm (8 x 5in).

2 Wrap a couple of pieces tightly around a straight jar, leaving a 5cm (2in) overlap at the bottom.

3 Fold the excess newspaper in across the bottom of the jar and stamp it on a hard surface to settle the newspaper in position.

4 Carefully pull the jar out of the newspaper mould and fold the top inwards to help keep the pot straight.

5 Fill with slightly damp compost and push the seeds into the soil. Prepare several pots and stand them on a rigid surface, such as a wooden seed tray, or a plate, and keep the soil moist until the seedlings emerge. Then plant out the newspaper pots intact.

Which crops to grow from seed

Depending on where you live, there are thousands of different vegetables in just as many varieties. I suggest you experiment – you will soon find out what suits your soil, your climate and your patience. To avoid gluts of the same foods, sow as wide a variety as possible, and try to plant crops that can be harvested at different times of the year. It is also wise to choose those vegetables and fruits that are expensive to buy as well as, of course, the ones that you are particularly fond of.

The following can be grown from seed in the garden or in pots on your balcony or window sill:

Vegetables:
artichokes
asparagus
aubergines
beetroot
borlotti beans
broad beans
broccoli
Brussels sprouts
cabbages
carrots
cauliflower
celeriac
celery
courgettes
cucumbers
fennel
French beans

garlic
Jerusalem artichokes
kale
kohl rabi
leeks
lettuce
marrows
onions
parsnips
peas
peppers
potatoes
pumpkins
radishes
runner beans
shallots
spring onions
sprouting broccoli

squash
swedes
sweet potatoes
sweetcorn
tomatoes
turnips

Fruit:
blackcurrants
blueberries
gooseberries
grapes
raspberries
redcurrants
rhubarb
strawberries
whitecurrants

BELOW: *A good crop of peppers can be raised in growbags as they require very little space.*

BELOW LEFT: *A fine aubergine plant, successfully grown in a pot.*

BOTTOM: *The beautiful veined leaves of a common cabbage – perfect leaves with absolutely no help from pesticides.*

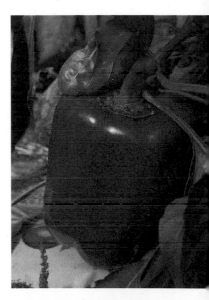

Flowering plants from seed

The variety of flowers that you can grow is limited only by your imagination. The three species of flowers that I grow abundantly in my garden are roses, sweet peas and lavender. These are generous in their provision of cut flowers, simple to grow and undemanding in their need for attention. Although we are often given plants and seedlings by friends and neighbours, I still enjoy the thrill of buying unusual varieties from local nurseries.

Enormous garden centres are popping up all over the place but I find them soulless, homogenized and uninspiring, with rank upon rank of identical perfect plants, imported mostly from abroad. Again, as with most of what is available to buy, it is better by far to support local growers partly because the indigenous species they grow will thrive, but mainly because they are a dying breed – as long as there are huge supermarket-like nurseries cornering the market, supplying cheap but ordinary alternatives, their livelihoods and expert knowledge are in danger of disappearing.

TOP LEFT: *At the end of the flowering season, collect seedheads for drying. The bunches can be hung upside down, with the heads enclosed in a paper bag to collect the seeds as they drop. Alternatively, gently shake the seedheads inside a paper bag. Store the seeds in clearly labelled envelopes, ready for planting next season.*

RIGHT: *Throughout the season, keep cutting sweetpea flowers to prevent seedheads forming and using up valuable energy. One packet of seeds can keep the house in flowers for the whole summer.*

BOTTOM LEFT: *Sunflowers attract wildlife, which consume unwanted pests.*

Growing from cuttings

So much money can be saved if you propagate your own plants by taking cuttings. It is terribly easy and most gratifying. If you have no garden, invest time in taking cuttings that can grow on your windowsill. Swap your time and effort for garden space with someone who can grow on your cuttings and provide you with the fruits of your joint labour.

The best time to take cuttings is in spring or summer when plants have new, vigorous, leafy growth. There are a variety of ways to propagate from cuttings, each with its own requirements. As a general rule, cuttings need adequate light, warmth and moisture. Avoid taking very small cuttings because they tend to exhaust their food reserves before their roots are formed.

A free-draining compost capable of retaining sufficient moisture will encourage the cuttings to form roots. Buy good-quality compost because using a sterilized medium prevents diseases from being passed on to vulnerable new plants.

Taking root

Some plants root easily if the cuttings are placed in water. Basil stems placed in a vase of water grow roots quickly, and the rooted cuttings can then be planted to create a good basil crop. Hormone rooting powder is very helpful when taking cuttings as the organic compounds hasten the formation of roots, creating sturdier plants in a shorter time.

Woody-stemmed plants, such as lavender, box, philadelphus and geraniums, are ideal for taking cuttings from. All of these plants have the added benefit of creating a striking display when planted in quantity, such as box hedges surrounding beds, and whole borders of lavender.

ABOVE: *All the box plants in my garden are descended from three plants bought a quarter of a century ago.*

LEFT: *Plants grown from cuttings in abundance.*

taking cuttings

If you have a propagator, so much the better, but a deep seed tray will do just as well. Line it with newspaper before filling with soil.

You will need

Plant from which to take cuttings
Rooting powder
Old saucer
Newspaper
Cuttings tray

1 Cut the stem of a non-flowering shoot just below the place where the leaf is sprouting.

2 Remove the lowest leaves on the cut stem.

3 Pour some rooting powder into an old saucer and dip the base of the cutting first in water, then in the powder, making sure it is well coated.

4 Fill the cuttings tray with seed compost and smooth it over. Push the cutting into the soil and gently firm the earth around it. Plant several cuttings of the same species in the same cuttings tray, keeping them apart from each other. When they are tall enough to handle, plant them out either in the garden or in larger containers.

Seasonal guide to growing your own produce

This seasonal list will help you plan your garden month by month. As well as helpful advice on vegetables, there is information on growing fruits and flowers.

Spring

▶ Keep digging to prepare the soil, applying compost and manure and a good sprinkling of Epsom salts (see page 105).

▶ Start successional sowing of salad crops.

▶ Cover emerging shoots with fleece when there is danger of frost.

▶ Cut out discs of old carpet underlay and place around the stems of brassicas to deter cabbage rootfly.

▶ Sort out your seeds into months for sowing.

▶ Sow broad beans outside – the earlier they are sown the hardier they will be and less likely to be attacked by blackfly.

▶ Plant carrot and any other seeds suitable for early sowing, following instructions on the packets.

▶ Sow flower seeds, planting enough to supply the house with cut flowers and enough to give as gifts.

▶ Divide plants in the border to increase your stock and make more space.

▶ Organize plant swaps with friends and neighbours so that you can give away a surplus of particular plants and receive others that you lack.

▶ Where necessary, support plants with bamboo sticks firmly pushed into the ground. Do this before the plants start toppling over so that you are less likely to damage roots whilst inserting the sticks and can encourage plant growth in the right direction from the start.

▶ Regularly hoe between rows to keep the soil free of weeds.

▶ Earth up potatoes to encourage a good crop.

ABOVE: *Freshly pulled bunches of carrots – their sweet flavour is unlike anything bought from the supermarket.*

RIGHT: *If properly looked after, old garden tools will last many lifetimes.*

Summer

▶ Continue successional sowings of flowers and vegetables.

▶ Plant out tender vegetables and plants as soon as risk of frost has passed.

▶ Plan time off, so that you can make full use of your crops when they are ready to be frozen or made into pies, jams, jellies and chutneys.

▶ Regularly dead head roses to encourage flowering.

▶ Watch out for greenfly, blackfly and other pests. On healthy, strong plants, use a hose to wash them off or wipe them off with a gloved hand.

▶ Encourage predators, such as ladybirds and hoverflies, by companion planting. (This involves growing pollen-rich flowering plants close to your vegetable plants to attract beneficial insects. Marigolds not only smell bad to aphids but attract hoverflies, which feed on aphids. Companion plants can also be used to entice away destructive pests from crops. For example, nasturtiums are easy to grow from seed and a popular companion plant to cabbages and lettuces because they attract caterpillars.) Pesticides made from insecticidal soap or rape seed oil are also available.

▶ To rid plants of greenfly and blackfly, boil torn-up rhubarb leaves in an old saucepan set aside for the purpose, and use the liquid to spray affected plants. This insecticide contains oxalic acid which is poisonous to greenfly and to man, so spray only onto non-edible plants as a last resort.

▶ In late summer, harvest crops such as onions and shallots, leaving them to dry in the sun.

▶ Plan the storage and use of crops. Make sure you have the ingredients and the wherewithal to pot jams and jellies, chutneys and pickles.

▶ Cut herbs and dry them to ensure a stock throughout the winter.

LEFT: *Onions need to be perfectly dry before storing.*

- Continue to feed and weed the soil, and continue planting throughout the season.
- Dig up perennial weeds, such as dandelions and docks, completely removing the roots from the soil. A three-year-old dandelion left to seed will produce around 5,000 weeds. A stitch in time …
- At first sight of bindweed dig gently down to its root, remove carefully and destroy. This weed has the ability to set down roots from just a tiny piece of carelessly left stem. Vigilance and instant removal is the only organic method for keeping your garden clear of this virulent weed. Never put bindweed on the compost heap – put it on the bonfire.
- Spraying neat vinegar onto weeds growing in difficult-to-access places such as between paving stones, will get rid of them permanently.
- Remember to stop and savour the beauty of your garden.

LEFT: *To kill weeds that are difficult to remove between cracks in paving, treat with neat vinegar.*

Autumn

▶ Lift and store vegetables before the first frosts arrive.
▶ Tidy fallen leaves and other debris, collecting sticks and pine cones for firelighters.
▶ Continue with the harvest, preserving and freezing produce.
▶ Cut and freeze or dry herbs for use during the winter.
▶ Plant winter salad crops in pots to grow on the windowsill.
▶ Check your apples in storage and remove any that are showing signs of deterioration immediately.

Winter

▶ On fine days begin digging the border and the vegetable patch.
▶ Keep checking stored vegetables and fruit, and remove any that are not healthy.
▶ Protect tender plants with fleece.
▶ Prune fruit trees and roses.
▶ Plant bare-rooted shrubs and trees.
▶ Check your apples in storage and immediately remove any that are showing signs of deterioration.
▶ Send for seed catalogues and plan your planting.
▶ You can continue to harvest winter crops such as swedes, parsnips, Brussels sprouts, leeks and cabbages.

BELOW: *Coloured lettuces planted together for dramatic effect.*

- Keep turning your compost heap.
- If you have bought a Christmas tree growing in a pot, it would be kind to re-pot it into a larger pot and feed it. Leave it outside until next Christmas.
- Winter is a good time to clean and sort out the potting shed, and prepare pots and seed trays. Disinfect them with a solution of distilled white vinegar and warm water.
- Clean tools and wipe them down with a rag dipped in olive oil.
- Sharpen cutting tools and then wipe with an olive oil rag.
- Clean and disinfect the greenhouse using non-toxic substances, such as distilled white vinegar or borax.

BELOW: *A variety of plants, grown from cuttings, taking shelter by the wall of the garden shed.*

Water

Without it we can't eat; with too much of it we can't eat. Last year we suffered from drought, this year we were inundated with flash floods, so it is hard to know exactly what will become of the weather. Until recently we were 'threatened' with Mediterranean summers and it was supposed that we would have to replace turnips with olive trees; the reality this year was very different. I think we have learned our lesson – not to believe anyone's predictions about the weather. No one really knows the extent of the damage we have done to our Earth's atmosphere and the effects that we will have to learn to live with, so practically we should prepare ourselves for all eventualities. I am writing this chapter in autumn and have just seen a branch of one of my apple trees in blossom – if trees think it is spring, imagine how confused I am! I also know of a hawthorn tree that is so confused it is bearing blossom, berries and new leaf as well as old all at the same time. Nature's confusion should be considered as a gentle warning to us.

Lawns and flowerbeds

Before the onset of 'decking mania', heavy rain was accommodated by lawns and flowerbeds. Now the water just runs off into drains and heavy downpours combined with thousands of decked gardens result in huge quantities of water overwhelming the drainage systems.

   Lesson number one – reinstate your lawn and your flowerbeds to slow down the water run-off. It is true that cutting the lawn is one less job when the whole garden is covered in decking, but tending a lawn – keeping it perfectly groomed and weed free – can become a bit of a healthy obsession. Flowerbeds might seem hard work compared to pots but, on the whole, looking after a small flowerbed is less work than looking after pots. For a start, when it does rain there are deeper reserves in the soil than there are in pots, and there is so much more choice in planting a border. From flowers for cutting to vegetables and fruit, there is so much more scope to be self-sufficient with a flowerbed.

RIGHT: *Using a watering can rather than a hose makes us more aware of how valuable each drop of water is.*

Collecting rainwater

If we presume there will be water shortage, it makes sense to accept the gifts provided by the heavens and store rainwater. Water butts and storage tanks provide a good supply, but you can let your imagination run wild and construct ponds, reservoirs, gullies and rills to use the water with decorative effect. Clever planting can disguise ugly water-collection containers or you can buy beautiful vintage containers at markets or auctions. Try to avoid the use of electric pumps to keep water flowing, as this defeats the green purpose. However, to avoid mosquitoes becoming a problem, keep standing water away from areas where people sit, eat and play. By clever planting of ponds, you can encourage wildlife, such as toads and frogs, which will eat the flies and mosquitoes.

Making the most of water

It is important to water plants efficiently, and there is much that can be done to preserve and protect plants during periods of drought.

- Make sure your soil's structure is as good as it can be, with adequate additions of organic compost to all soils, sand to heavy clay soils, etc.
- Install a water butt to collect rainwater, and make sure your gutters are clear of leaves and debris for good flow.
- Mulch plants with a good layer of wood chip or bark, which not only conserves moisture but suppresses weeds.
- Keep flowerbeds free from weeds, which compete with your plants for nutrients and water reserves.
- Watering with a watering can makes us aware of the precious nature of each drop. Pour the water directly onto the roots.
- Always water during the early morning or in the evening when your efforts won't be wasted by the drying effects of the sun.
- Choose plants that are suited to your environment – it makes life so much less complicated.
- Use water-retaining granules, which conserve water and release it slowly.
- Investigate re-plumbing your home to make good use of 'grey' water. Bath water and washing-up water that does not contain any toxic chemicals can be used to water plants. This method of watering is best kept for flowering plants rather than food plants.
- Invest in a clever invention – 'WaterGreen', a very simple gadget invented by Louise Angus and Antonia Lord (see page 187). Nothing more than a simple hand-squeeze pump, it turns a hose into a siphon that drains bath water effortlessly through the hose pipe to any place that is lower than the bath. As long as only natural unguents and bath preparations are used, the 'grey' bath water can be re-directed to the garden below.

RIGHT: *Water roses at their roots in the early morning or at dusk so that water does not evaporate and to ensure a continuous supply of blooms.*

Feeding plants and shrubs

As well as home-made organic compost, a major, but little known asset to the gardener's store cupboard is a good supply of Epsom salts. Their beautifying and health-giving properties are listed in Chapter Five (see page 167), but the benefits of this completely natural compound to the garden are also numerous – I cannot recommend Epsom salts highly enough. A generation ago, they were frequently used in the garden and in the medicine cupboard, but Epsom salts seem to have fallen by the wayside in recent years, replaced by more 'up-to-date' chemical formulae, many of which cause more harm to the garden than good.

Studies have shown that magnesium and sulphur (two of the components of Epsom salts), enrich the soil to benefit vegetable crops and flowering plants.

The benefits of using Epsom salts include:

▶ Helping seeds to germinate.

▶ Promoting bushier plant growth.

▶ Encouraging flowering plants to produce more flowers.

▶ Increasing chlorophyll production in plants.

▶ Improving the phosphorus and nitrogen uptake of plants.

LEFT: *Container gardening on a grand scale – feed pots regularly and remove dead flowerheads to keep the display healthy and ensure continuous flowering.*

How Epsom salts work

Crop research has found that magnesium is a vital mineral for seed germination and helps plants to produce chlorophyll, which transforms sunlight into food. Magnesium also helps plants to absorb phosphorus and nitrogen, two major fertilizer components. Sulphur is also an important plant nutrient, promoting chlorophyll production.

Although magnesium and sulphur occur naturally in the soil, they can be depleted by factors such as excessive rainfall and heavy agricultural use. Unlike most commercial fertilizers, which build up in the soil over time, Epsom salts are not persistent so cannot be overused. Tests by the National Gardening Association show that roses fertilized with Epsom salts are much healthier, grow much bushier and produce more flowers than those treated with commercial fertilizer.

Epsom salts can be used to encourage leaf growth on fruit and vegetables, such as tomatoes, lettuce, broccoli, cauliflower, cabbages and other brassicas, and to promote leaf growth and plentiful flowers on shrubs, flowering plants and fruit trees. Apply the salts every 4–6 weeks throughout the growing season from spring until early autumn.

Dissolve four handfuls into 10 litres (about 18 pints) of water – this quantity will drench a 15 square metre (about 50 square feet) plot. Alternatively, sprinkle around the roots of plants and water in.

When planting new rose trees and bushes, sprinkle a handful into the newly dug hole before planting. Apart from compost and manure, the only substance I use to encourage growth in my garden is Epsom salts.

ABOVE: *At Cabbages & Roses, we package Epsom salts in tins made from ecologically sound metals.*

BELOW: *Use water in which eggs have been boiled to water plants – this will give them much-appreciated calcium.*

ACID-LOVING PLANTS

To water acid-loving plants such as azaleas, mix one cup of vinegar to 4.5 litres (1 gallon) of water. Immerse plants in buckets containing this solution until the water stops bubbling.

comfrey fertilizer

Comfrey leaves contain allantoin, an agent that stimulates healthy tissue formation, and for this reason comfrey is used in medical treatments and beauty preparations. The leaves can also be used to make a very effective natural fertilizer. Grow a patch in the garden for a continuous supply.

you will need

Comfrey leaves
Enamel bucket
Heavy stone
Water
Funnel
Bottle

1 Collect enough leaves to layer nearly to the top of an enamel bucket and place a heavy stone on top of them.

2 Add 600ml (1 pint) of water and leave to rot in a warm place for about a month.

3 Drain the liquid from the bucket and store in a clean, labelled bottle. Using a funnel makes it easier.

4 To use, make a solution of one part comfrey liquid to four parts water and feed it to growing plants of all kinds.

Garden pests

The battle against pests in the garden is never ending, making it very tempting to resort to toxic chemicals. However, apart from being unkind – I hate the thought of even a slug dying a slow and painful death – it should not be necessary to use toxic substances when there are other methods that are just as effective.

Organic farmers control both disease and pests by clever planting (see pages 114–115), and by encouraging the wildlife species that are the natural predators of the pests that we spend so much time, money and greenhouse gases trying to eliminate. Nature has a balance and, if left to her own devices, will manage to feed wildlife and mankind, as long as we show her the respect she deserves.

Natural pest control

All the natural methods of pest control that follow are as adequate as their chemical counterparts. Unlike commercial pesticides, they do not harm the natural predators of pests or the environment.

One of the most effective ways to prevent infestation is to grow strong, healthy plants. In my experience, these can survive an occasional attack from small pests if you are vigilant and react quickly.

Slugs and snails

Humane snail and slug traps Make humane traps for snails and slugs by burying bowls of beer in the soil, pouring in enough beer to drown a decent-sized slug. The enticing odour of the beer will attract the pests so that they slither into the bowl, get drunk and drown. Milk and water is an alternative lure, but I prefer the idea of a drunk slug drowning to the rather sweet idea of a slug with milk whiskers. Humane traps are an infinitely kinder method of ridding the garden of one of its most irritating pests than using toxic slug pellets, which are eaten by slugs, and the slugs in turn are eaten by birds.

Remember to empty the traps often and renew the beer – this is not a pleasant task but infinitely preferable to the disappointment of watching all your hard work in the garden disappear in a slime trail.

Many beneficial beetles, ladybirds etc also get murdered by these "traps"...

RIGHT: *Avoid slug damage to hostas by planting in a pot rather than in the ground. Apply a thick layer of petroleum jelly around the top of the pot to prevent the slugs entering.*

Snail and slug deterrents Snails and slugs dislike slithering over sharp, gritty materials so put layers of wood ash around tender emerging plants, especially hostas, which are favoured by slugs. Renew after rainfall.

Sharp Christmas tree branches laid around seedlings will protect plants for a while. However, the branches need to be renewed as rainfall softens the ground and buries the needles. Dry, crushed eggshells have the same effect. *Try coffee grounds, usually free from Starbucks, Costa, etc*

To prevent snails and slugs climbing up pots to eat your plants, apply a thick layer of petroleum jelly around the pot about 2.5cm (1in) from the top. This method can also be used around holes in tree bark. Copper tape also deters the creatures from getting near your seedlings.

Slug-eating wildlife Encourage wildlife, such as birds and hedgehogs, which will feast on slugs. Pesticides, slug pellets and loss of habitat are the biggest threats to these natural slug predators. Welcome hedgehogs into your garden by making shelters out of dried leaves and twigs. Put food out for them at dusk so that flies will not be attracted to it. Check the food in the morning and, if it has not been eaten, dispose of it immediately. Hedgehogs can be fed on peanut butter or chopped peanuts, vegetables and raw or cooked meat. Never put out milk for hedgehogs – they will drink it but it is bad for their health in many ways. Before lighting bonfires or cutting long grass, check that you are not disturbing a hedgehog nest.

Weeding
Weeds can encourage disease in plants of the same species – for instance, shepherd's purse and charlock are members of the brassica family. If they are harbouring club root, this can be passed on to your cabbage crop.

Rhubarb
Many small pests dislike the presence of rhubarb, so use it as a companion plant (see page 114). Placing a piece of fresh rhubarb in the planting hole of cabbage seedling deters rootfly from moving in. (A piece of carpet underlay serves the same purpose.) You might also want to use rhubarb water (the water rhubarb has been cooked in) to water all members of the brassica family.

Netting
Use netting to protect small seedlings from birds. Fruit trees also benefit from being covered with netting. If birds are denied the opportunity to feast on your fruits, they are more likely to opt for an alternative diet of slugs and flies.

BELOW: Rhubarb – for eating and for pest control.

Protecting fruit trees

Tie corrugated cardboard around the trunks of fruit trees in late summer. It will provide a home for a variety of fruit-tree pests, such as moth grubs and weevils. Remove the cardboard after a week or two and destroy; start again with new cardboard.

Crop rotation

To keep soil healthy, crop rotation is an essential part of organic gardening. This is because each crop tends to leach the soil of a particular nutrient. Planting the same crop over and over again will exhaust the soil of that nutrient. Crop rotation allows the balance of nutrients to re-establish, and prevents pests and diseases particular to specific crops from building up in the soil. Never plant the same crop in the same bed for two years running. Keep planting plans from year to year because it is very easy to forget which plant has been grown in which bed.

BELOW: *A home-made cage, created from recycled wood and wire mesh, protects a crop from pests.*

Attracting beneficial insects

Some companion plants (see pages 114–115) not only deter particular crop pests but also attract the insects that feed on them. Planting specific shrubs to attract butterflies, hoverflies and bees adds to the beauty of the garden and, by encouraging the right sort of wildlife, you are dealing with the wrong – damaging – sort. Shrubs require little effort and some are also generous in providing cut flowers for the house.

SHRUBS FOR WELCOMING WILDLIFE

Butterfly bush (*Buddleia davidii*)   Lavender (*Lavandula*)
Common ivy (*Hedera helix*)   Lilac (*Syringa* x *hyacinthiflora*)
Escallonia   Privet (*Ligustrum quihoui*)
Heather (*Calluna vulgaris*)   Blackberry (*Rubus*)
Firethorn (*Pyracantha*)   Sage (*Salvia officinalis*)
Hebe (*Hebe albicans*)   Thyme (*Thymus vulgaris*)

Bees: the gardener's friend

It is thought that there are 30,000 different species of bees in the world, and one third of our food supplies depends on pollination by bees and other insects. Encourage bees to visit your garden by planting blue, white, yellow and purple flowers for their ultraviolet properties.

Honey from bees living close to urban environments is far more delicious than honey from hives in farmland. This is because of the variety of flowers producing the nectar that flavours honey; acres of the same crop create no variety.

Ladybirds

Encourage ladybirds into your garden as they eat greenfly and blackfly. Ladybirds like to lay eggs in nettles, so leaving a small nettle patch to flourish in your garden should increase ladybird numbers. One ladybird that lives for one year can eat more than 5,000 aphids. If a plant is infested with aphids, don't panic and spray it with a chemical pesticide – once ladybirds reach that plant they will eat the aphids quickly. If there is no sign of ladybirds dealing with the problem, spray with a strong jet of water from a hose to wash them off.

RIGHT: *Lavender thrives in dry, sunny spots and will encourage wildlife into the garden.*

TIPS FOR OTHER GARDEN PESTS AND DISEASES

Mildew
To cure mildew on gooseberries, spray the plants with one part water and one part milk.

Blackfly and greenfly
If your strong, healthy plants are infested with blackfly or greenfly, wash off the pests rather than killing them with pesticides. Spray water directly from a hose without a fitting on the end, putting your finger on the hose outlet to control the strength of the water jet.

Moles
To deter moles from digging holes in your garden leaving unsightly, although useful, crumbly earth, bury plastic bottles in the ground leaving about 2.5cm (1in) of the bottle neck exposed. The noise from the wind blowing across the top of the bottle neck will deter the moles. You can use glass bottles, but I feel this might be dangerous if you should forget about them being there and mow them accidentally. Another deterrent for moles is to put fresh garlic cloves into their holes.

Protecting seeds
Prevent the seeds of peas and beans planted outside from being eaten by birds, mice or rabbits by covering with chicken wire secured by pegs.

BELOW LEFT: *Ladybirds are one of nature's best defences against aphids.*

BELOW: *Nettles growing wild are a good source of nutrients for both humans and plants, and encourage ladybirds.*

Companion planting

This is a time-tested method of deterring pests without the use of chemicals. Frequently it is the aromatic foliage or flowers of the companion plant that either deter the pest or entice it away from the main crop plants – effectively acting as a decoy.

VEGETABLE/FRUIT	PLANT NEXT TO OR NEAR:
asparagus	basil, parsley
aubergines	broad beans, marigolds
broad beans	celery, cucumbers, strawberries
cabbages	beetroot, celery, chamomile and other herbs, onions, rhubarb

BELOW: My vegetable patch – all the box hedging has been grown from cuttings from three plants bought 25 years ago.

VEGETABLE/FRUIT	PLANT NEXT TO OR NEAR:
carrots	lettuces, marigolds, onions, tomatoes
celery	cabbages, onions, nasturtiums, tomatoes
cucumbers	beans, peas, radishes, sunflowers
lettuce and salad crops	radishes, strawberries
onions	cabbage, carrots, lettuce
peas	beans, carrots, cucumbers, sweetcorn
potatoes	cabbages, marigolds, sweetcorn
pumpkins	marigolds, sweetcorn
radishes	cucumbers, lettuce, peas, nasturtiums
runner beans	radishes, sweetcorn
spinach	cauliflowers, celery, strawberries
squash	marigolds, sweetcorn
strawberries	broad beans, lettuces, onions, spinach
sweetcorn	broad beans, cucumbers, potatoes,
tomatoes	asparagus, carrots, marigolds, parsley

HERBS AS COMPANION PLANTS

Planted in combination with crops, herbs are also extremely effective at repelling specific insects and pests.

HERB	PLANT NEXT TO OR NEAR:
basil	tomatoes
bay leaves	beans
borage	strawberries, tomatoes
catnip	aubergines
chamomile	cabbages, onions
chives	carrots
coriander	all vegetables
dill	cabbages
feverfew	roses
garlic	raspberries, roses
hyssop	cabbages
mint	cabbages, tomatoes
nasturtium	cabbages, pumpkins, radishes
oregano	brassicas
rosemary	beans, cabbages, carrots
sage	cabbages, carrots
thyme	cabbages

TOP RIGHT: *green tomatoes on the vine*; CENTRE: *pumpkins and squash*;
BOTTOM: *broad beans – all are ideal crops for companion planting.*

CHAPTER 4

THE WELL-STOCKED LARDER

Much of what we buy from a supermarket has travelled on average 20,000 kilometres (12,500 miles). One day we might find ourselves in the situation where oil has become so extortionately expensive that the idea of our food travelling so far to reach our plates is ludicrous (even without oil being prohibitively expensive, the idea is ludicrous). We might find our plates empty unless we rediscover the skills needed to produce food ourselves, locally, organically, safely and sustainably. Whether we are growing food ourselves or we are shopping for food, it would be an enormous contribution to lessening the effects of global warming if we were, as much as we possibly can, to shop locally, seasonally and organically.

Local producers and supermarkets

I have to admit that I often find myself in a supermarket. I am not suggesting that supermarkets are an expendable commodity – they have a place in our time-restricted lives. However, more consideration should be taken as to where they are allowed, the way they treat their suppliers and the damage they do to the custom of smaller, local shops. I do believe that the resurgence of specialist food shops and farmers' markets is proving that we do understand that eating seasonal, locally produced food is an important factor in reducing our carbon footprint.

LEFT, BELOW AND RIGHT: *Supermarket packaging is responsible for 4.6 million tons of waste generated every year in the UK alone. It is us who buy and dispose of the packaging and it is therefore up to us to stop buying such over-packaged produce. Produce bought at farmers' markets is usually wrapped in paper or placed straight into your shopping basket or bag.*

For me, buying food from a supermarket is something I am not proud of since I am fortunate enough to live in an area surrounded by farmers' markets and locally run farm shops, and I grow my own fruit and vegetables. Like many others, I justify my actions by a shortage of time and a scatty head full of deadlines. My failing eyesight renders me completely blind to the tiny writing on packaging. Even last week I bought broccoli wrapped in plastic, flown in from Spain – I blush with shame as I write. There is spinach, lettuce, chard and asparagus in my garden. I wanted to buy lamb but, searching the meat cabinet for an English flag, I could find only imports from New Zealand. I asked an assistant why, in this corner of England, surrounded by farmland particularly suited to rearing sheep, did they not stock English lamb? The reply: 'We are having difficulty finding a supply.'

Seasonal food

Whether you live in a city, a town, a suburb or in the country, there should always be a supply of indigenous food – we only have to look for it, or to ask for it. The time has come for us to realize the impact of having non-seasonal produce in our shops, and of imported food replacing what we can grow easily on our own doorstep.

To wait for the local strawberry season is not a hardship. We should and must ask ourselves whether a bowl of strawberries flown in from the other side of the world is a necessary extravagance. Apart from the air miles, the electricity used in keeping the fruits fresh and the enormous task of distribution from central storage areas, more often than not they are tasteless. This summer a supermarket giant was selling strawberries flown in, the label proudly announced, from the USA – halfway across the world to provide us with strawberries which are grown in abundance not 32km (20 miles) from the shop. I do not question the high quality of the American strawberries; I do question the fact that supermarket fruit buyers don't seem to understand the huge impact their buying strategies are having on our world – all in the name of commerce.

The traditional larder

To make use of seasonal foods, a good larder is essential if you are to survive without daily trips to the supermarket. Position the larder in a northerly aspect of your home if possible, and keep it dark, cool and well ventilated. A slate shelf is traditionally installed for storing items that need to be kept cool rather than refrigerator cold. It is also invaluable for cooling cooked dishes before putting them in the fridge. Remember that putting warm or hot food in the fridge uses a great deal of electricity to return it to its right temperature. If your larder's proportions are unsuitable for installing a slate cold shelf, think about positioning one in the garage or a garden shed.

   Another solution is to build or buy a traditional meat safe – simply a wooden cupboard with wire mesh on the door to allow airflow. This could prove to be an invaluable asset, especially at Christmas time when the fridge is usually full to overflowing, and the cold winter air is perfectly adequate for storing foods such as cheeses and vegetables. It can be kept in a cool garage or outhouse, but make sure pets (or vermin) cannot access its contents.

Store cupboard ingredients
Keep your larder stocked with the following:

Necessities for preserving:
- vinegar
- sugar
- sea salt
- spices
- dried herbs
- collection of recycled jam jars

For rainy days and hungry guests:
- dried beans – broad, chickpeas, flageolet, haricot
- dried fruit – apricots, currants, raisins, etc
- jars and jars of home-made jams, jellies, chutneys and pickles
- organic cooking chocolate (in industrial quantities)
- organic flour
- organic oats – for cooking, baking and bathing
- organic pasta – a good selection of sizes and shapes
- organic tomatoes – tinned or bottled
- organic dried yeast

Produce to grow in huge quantities because it stores well:
- apples
- beetroot
- garlic
- nuts
- onions and shallots
- potatoes
- soft fruits
- tomatoes – to use fresh, in chutneys or in sauces

Food items to buy when you don't know what to buy:
- lemons – for a million reasons
- organic butter
- organic eggs
- organic milk and cream

Harvesting and storing

The most important rule in the storing of produce, whether bought or grown yourself, is to store only perfect fruits and vegetables. When harvesting, separate any damaged fruit of vegetables and use immediately; dispose of anything that looks infected on the bonfire. Perfect specimens are less likely to deteriorate in storage and more likely to keep for months.

Pick vegetables at their optimum size – the younger, the better – over a period of time. The aim is to avoid finding yourself picking old, stringy vegetables or gigantic peas as the effort involved in preserving them will be rather wasted. Remember that the more young, succulent vegetables you pick, the more the plant will respond by producing more.

Storing vegetables

When the garden is producing more than you and your family can eat, try these storage methods for putting food by for winter months.

Beans and peas

Dry and store beans and peas, or blanch them in lightly salted water and freeze. To blanch, bring a pan of water to the boil, add the vegetables and bring back to the boil for one minute. Drain and plunge them immediately into ice-cold water, and drain again – this will preserve their beautiful bright green colour. Shake them dry, then seal them in bags and put into the freezer immediately.

Garlic

As with onions, it is important to store dry, perfect specimens. If they are less than perfect, use straight away. Keeping the long stalks intact provides the perfect method of storage. Once you have plaited the stalks together into a long rope, hang in a cool, dark place.

Onions

Harvest onions when most of the tops have fallen over and begun to wilt and dry. Pull or dig the bulbs out carefully with the tops attached. After harvesting, dry or cure the onions in a warm, dry, well-ventilated location,

A WELL-STOCKED FREEZER
One of the few modern-day inventions that can make up for its carbon footprint in its usefulness is the freezer. Well stocked and efficiently run it can save many a trip to the supermarket. It is also invaluable for storing seasonal fruit and vegetables from the garden or from the market, to keep you fed throughout the winter months.

dried apple rings

This is a simple yet effective way to store apples for cooking. The dried apple rings can be kept for use throughout the winter, and are ideal for pies and apple sauces.

you will need
Apples (with no bruises)
Apple corer and sharp knife
Sturdy string
Freezer bag

1 Using only perfect fruit with no bruising, peel and core the apples. Then slice them to make rings 5mm–1cm (¼–½in) thick.

2 Thread the apple rings onto a length of sturdy string and hang them in a warm, dry place.

3 When the apple rings are perfectly dry, seal them in a plastic bag, making sure all the air is expelled, and store them in a cool, dark cupboard.

4 When you come to use them, put them in a saucepan with a small amount of water, bring to the boil and simmer until they are re-constituted. Then include them in your recipe as you would fresh apples.

such as a shed or garage. If the weather is sunny, leave onions outside to dry but cover them at night so they don't get damp in the morning dew.

Cure the onions for two to four weeks until the tops and necks are thoroughly dry and the outer bulb scales begin to rustle. After the onions are properly cured, cut off the tops about 2.5cm (1in) above the bulbs. As you top the onions, discard any that show signs of decay. Use the thick-necked bulbs immediately as they don't store well.

Place the cured onions in a mesh bag, wicker basket, wire basket or a crate (or plait them together so that they can be hung) and store them in a cool, dry location such as a garage, potting shed, larder or cold room. In particularly cold climes, the temperature in an unheated garage or shed may fall well below freezing. If such extreme weather is expected, bring the onions inside until the temperature rises.

The storage life of onions is determined by the variety and storage conditions. Good keepers, such as 'Sweet Sandwich', that are properly stored should keep for several months. Onions will sprout if the storage temperatures are too warm and they may deteriorate in damp locations.

Although onions are easy to grow and it is satisfying to store enough to cover your needs for several months, they are also cheap and easy to buy, so I wouldn't get too stressed about their storage.

Root crops

The traditional method of storing root crops, such as potatoes, parsnips and beetroot, is known as clamping. It involves making a pyramid from straw and earth beaten flat with the back of a shovel. However, in this day and age we can probably manage with other, less arduous methods. Sturdy paper potato sacks are adequate for storing root vegetables and are easily obtainable. Vegetables stored in this manner must be dry and in perfect condition at the outset. Store in cool, dry and dark conditions – a cold store, north-facing larder or a garage are all perfect locations.

Sweetcorn

Boil sweetcorn in water for 15 minutes, then dry in a slow oven overnight. Cut the kernels off the cobs, seal them in jars and store in a cool, dark larder. To use them, just boil in salted water until tender.

LEFT: *If you leave the long stalks on drying onions and garlic, they can be plaited together to make a long string (start plaiting from the bulb end) and hung in a cool place to store.*

RIGHT: *Store only perfect specimens of potato, make sure they are dry and kept in a dark, cool place. Never eat potatoes with green areas – this is caused by storing potatoes in the light.*

Storing fruit

Although the best option is always to eat fruit fresh from the garden, part of the pleasure of growing your own crops, or buying seasonally during the short window of excess, is that you can store a good supply for the dreary winter months.

At certain times of year the garden is laden with goodies. In the summer, strawberries, blackcurrants, redcurrants, loganberries and raspberries are almost overwhelmingly plentiful. Later in the year, apples, crab apples, pears and quinces become abundant.

Apples

You can store apples for as long as four months, but each fruit must be in good condition with no sign of bruising or insect damage. Wrap each one separately in newspaper (the black-and-white pages, not the colour supplements) to prevent any mould or bacteria from spreading. Store in special wooden apple racks or baskets in a cool, dry, dark place. Early-ripening varieties are best used straight away. You can also dry apples cut into rings – see page 123 for details.

LEFT: *Wrap each apple individually in newspaper to prevent the spread of disease.*

RIGHT: *Ripe apples, ready for picking and storing for winter use.*

STORING NUTS

Due to their high fat content, nuts are susceptible to going rancid so the best way to store shelled nuts is in sealed jars or bags, kept in the freezer. This does them no harm and they will keep for up to eight months. Nuts easily absorb odours from their surroundings – another reason for keeping them in isolation in cold storage. Always taste stored nuts before using them because, if they have turned rancid, they will spoil the entire dish.

Soft fruits

Soft fruits can be stewed, made into pies, jellies, jams and cordials, or frozen. Soft fruits, such as blackcurrants, blackberries, gooseberries and raspberries, respond well to freezing. Firstly inspect each fruit, removing leaves and creatures, and wipe clean. Discard any bad or damaged fruits and either use immediately or put on the compost heap. Spread out fruits on a flat baking pan or tray that will fit into the freezer easily. Freeze in batches, making sure each fruit lies separately. It will not take very long to freeze these little individual fruits and, when they are solid, they can be decanted into bags and stored.

If gathering blackberries from roadside bushes, before using soak them for five minutes in a solution of cold water to which two tablespoons of distilled white vinegar have been added. This will remove the effects of road pollution.

LEFT: *Frozen raspberries are lovely in summer drinks. Used instead of ice cubes, they will flavour the drink as they slowly thaw.*

TOP RIGHT: *Straw placed under strawberry crops will deter slugs and keep the fruits clean during rainfall, preventing mud and dirt contaminating them.*

CENTRE RIGHT: *Raspberry bushes can provide fruit throughout the summer and well into autumn months across several different fruiting varieties.*

BOTTOM RIGHT: *Blackberries growing wild in the hedgerow.*

petal sugar

Flavoured sugars have all sorts of uses in cooking, and are an unusual – and delightful – addition to the larder. For instance, rose petal sugar can be added to soufflés, and the petals of sweet violet make a delicately scented sugar to sprinkle on cakes and pastries. Alternatively, herbs, such as rosemary, can be used as flavouring, and the versatile lavender has a distinctive taste. Make sure all herbs or flowers are clean, dry and untainted by chemical sprays before making the sugar.

you will need
Rose petals
Castor sugar
2 airtight jars
Sieve

1 In a clean, dry, airtight jar, alternate a layer of castor sugar with a layer of rose petals.

2 When the jar is full, close it and leave in a cool, dark larder for one to two weeks.

3 After that time, sieve the sugar to remove all traces of the petals or herbs.

4 Pour into another airtight jar, seal and return to the larder until you're ready to use it.

Preserves, jams, jellies and drinks

When you find yourself with a glut of fruit and want to preserve some of your crop, or when produce is in season and therefore cheaper, turn the excess into jam – jam making is a tradition well worth keeping alive. The pleasure you get from ranks of a mish mash of jam jars filled with jams, jellies and chutneys, shiny and dark, lined up in the larder is hard to measure.

Home-made preserves also make a lovely gift. In fact, any home-made gift is so much more meaningful than something bought in a shop. Once you have made jams, and look lovingly at the 'fruits' of your labour, it is indeed quite hard to give them away. A gift of home-made jam is so precious that you might become quite mean-spirited and need to think really hard about whether the recipient is deserving enough! A clever way around this mean-spiritedness is to make sure you keep a stock of very small jam jars – particularly sweet are the miniature versions of the 'Le Parfait' spring-lidded jars. It is easier to part with a little jar than a whopping great pot, especially if you have even the slightest doubt as to whether it will be truly appreciated.

To make up for that rather cruel and selfish last paragraph, may I suggest that a more interesting – not to mention generous – gift would be to present a selection of jams packed in a box.

The recipes for preserves in this chapter come from a variety of tried and tested sources. Mainly, they have been passed on to me by my mother who, in turn, inherited them from her mother. The secret to making preserves is to follow the recipes in minute detail, weigh the fruit, weigh the sugar and follow the timings.

STORAGE JARS

Le Parfait preserving jars are a good investment, and come in a variety of sizes. The jars are simpler to fill than standard ones because they are quite wide at the top; they also have a very satisfactory sealing mechanism. Although the rubber seals perish after a while, replacements are easily available from specialist cooking shops.

RIGHT: *The jewel-like hues of home-made jams and jellies – stored in the larder, they will see you through the winter months.*

Jam-making utensils

Preserving pan Although special equipment
is not really necessary for making preserves,
investing in a preserving pan will make the job
easier. These pans are wider at the top than at
the bottom, which makes the evaporation process
much quicker than in a normal saucepan, This
is especially useful for reducing vinegar when
making chutney. It is an investment that I
recommend – their handsome shape is an
incentive to make jam.

Jars Keep every jam jar with a lid that finds its
way into your house. Jam jars have all manner
of uses in the organic home – including storing
home-made jam. Jars need to be sterilized before
filling with preserves.

Sterilizing jars Half fill the jars with hot water
and place in a roasting pan. Add boiling water to
the pan to reach about a quarter of the way up
the jars; immerse the lids in the water. Put in a
moderate oven for about 10 minutes.

Jelly strainers Jellies need to be strained. You
can buy a jelly strainer from specialist cooking
shops, but I think they look rather disgusting
after use as it is difficult to wash them
satisfactorily when they have become stained
with fruit. They also need to be hung from a
height to drip into the bowl, which is not terribly
practical. Instead, invest in a large sieve and line
it with muslin or gauze – this is a much simpler
and less unruly method.

Wax discs These are available from stationers
or grocery shops. They provide a seal for the
preserves and are placed on top of the jam or
chutney before sealing with a lid.

RIGHT: *Kilner jars come in useful for storing a variety
of things, from jams to cleaning products.*

Useful hints for jam making

Preparing and selecting fruit Make sure the fruit you choose is dry and, if not, spread it out on a dry, clean tea towel and leave to dry. If the fruit is wet, the pectin naturally present in fruit will be diluted and the jam will not set satisfactorily. Under-ripe fruit contains more pectin and fruit acid, which helps the setting process, than over-ripe fruit, which is best avoided in jam making.

Lemon juice Add lemon juice to fruits that contain less pectin, such as strawberries.

Preserving sugar You can buy special preserving sugar with added pectin. Try it if you find that your jams are not setting well. This type of sugar is a little more expensive than ordinary sugar but does help with the setting process.

Equal quantities The general principle in jam making is to boil fruit to which its same weight in sugar has been added.

Testing the setting point Leave several saucers in the fridge to cool. When you think the jam is at setting point, spoon a little onto a cold saucer, and leave for a few minutes. If it forms a crinkled skin when pushed with your finger, the jam has reached setting point.

Potting Take the pan off the heat and fill the sterilized jars carefully. Cover the top of the jam with a waxed disc and seal with a lid. Store in a cool dark larder.

BELOW: *Sterilize all glass jars in a baking tray in the oven before filling with your home-made preserves.*

Strawberry jam

This recipe is good for using up a glut of fruit during the strawberry season. The jam will keep for several months.

1.8kg (4lb) slightly under-ripe dry strawberries, hulled
1.3kg (3lb) sugar or preserving sugar
Juice of 2 large lemons
10g (½oz) butter

Layer the hulled strawberries in a preserving pan with the sugar and leave overnight. By the morning the sugar will have almost dissolved. Shake the pan to distribute the fruit and juices. Place on low heat and without stirring too much (shake it a bit like professional cooks do) and wait until all the sugar has completely dissolved. At this point add the lemon juice and turn up the heat. When the jam has boiled for about 8 minutes, remove from the heat.

Meanwhile, chill a few saucers in the fridge, ready for testing the set. Sterilize six jam jars (see page 134).

To test for setting point, spoon a small amount of the jam onto a cold saucer; when cool, test to see whether a light skin has formed by pushing it with your finger. If it has, the jam is ready to be potted; if not, boil for a few minutes more, until the cold saucer test works.

Stir in the butter to disperse the scum that will probably have formed. Ladle the jam into the sterilized jars, place a wax disc on top of the jam and screw the lid on tight. The heat will form a good seal.

RIGHT: *A good crop of home-grown strawberries, collected in a fine jam pan.*

Gooseberry jam

Unless the gooseberries are particularly large, they don't need cutting up for this recipe.

1kg (2¼lb) green gooseberries
150ml (¼ pint) cold water
1kg (2¼lb) sugar

Place the gooseberries in a preserving pan or saucepan and stew gently with the water. When they are soft and tender, add the sugar and stir until it has completely dissolved. Boil rapidly until setting point is reached (see page 135). Pour into sterilized jars (see page 135) and seal.

Blackcurrant jam

Before making the jam, carefully pick over the fruit, removing stalks, leaves and any unwanted visitors.

1.8kg (4lb) ripe blackcurrants
600ml (1 pint) cold water
1.8kg (4lb) sugar

Place the fruit in a preserving pan with the water. Slowly bring to the boil and simmer gently for 30 minutes. Add the sugar and stir until it has dissolved. Continue to simmer for 15 minutes or until the jam reaches setting point (see page 135). Pour into sterilized jars (see page 135) and seal.

Medlar jam

Medlars are inedible until they start to decay. However, they will rarely reach this stage by themselves on the tree and need to be harvested. They should be left outside in a box until they turn a reddish-dark brown and have become soft, juicy and just on the point of rotting. In the seventeenth century this rotting process was known as 'bletting' the medlars. Serve this jam with cold meats.

450g (1lb) medlars, 'bletted'
750ml (1¼ pints) cold water
Sugar
Juice of 1 lemon

Weigh the medlars (the above measurements are a guide). Simmer the bletted medlars in the water until soft. Strain through a muslin-lined sieve or jelly bag. Measure the resulting juice and pour into a preserving pan. Add 450g (1lb) sugar to every 600ml (1 pint) of juice extracted from the fruit. Add the lemon juice and bring to the boil until setting point is reached (see page 135). Pot as normal (see page 135).

RIGHT: *A medlar fruit on the tree – too fresh to use at this stage, medlars must be bletted (see above) before turning into jam.*

Redcurrant jelly

Put the redcurrants into a preserving pan and gently heat until the berries have given up their juices. Empty into a sieve lined with fine gauze or a jelly bag and allow the juice to drip through. If you like your jellies to have a jewel-like transparency, don't be tempted to squash the fruit through as this will make your jelly cloudy. Personally I don't have the patience to wait and always end up squishing and pushing just to speed things up a little.

Measure the juice into a preserving pan, and add 450g (1lb) preserving sugar to every 600ml (1 pint) of juice extracted from the fruit. Stir over low heat until the sugar has dissolved completely. Bring to the boil and boil rapidly until setting point has been reached (see page 135). Pour into sterilized jars (see page 135).

Note: Once jellies have been made, before bottling add a handful of chopped herbs or whole sprigs of rosemary to the boiling juice just before decanting and sealing.

Crab apple jelly

Inspect the fruit and cut in half – there is no need to peel or core these fruits. Follow the recipe for redcurrant jelly (above) and for every 600ml (1 pint) of crab apple juice obtained, add 450g (1lb) preserving sugar.

Grape jelly

This recipe can use up the grapes that are really too small to eat.

Pick the grapes and remove from the stems. Place in a saucepan or preserving pan and place on a low heat. Stew until the fruits give up their juice, if necessary adding a small amount of water. Stir and mash with a wooden spoon to help the process along. Put the grape mush into a muslin-lined sieve over a large bowl and allow the juice to strain. Measure the juice and pour into the pan – for every 600ml (1 pint) of liquid, add 450g (1lb) sugar. Bring to the boil until setting point has been reached (see page 135). Pour into sterilized jars.

ABOVE LEFT: *Grapes – too small for eating – are ideal for turning into grape jelly.*

RIGHT: *Gigantic fruits from the quince tree, waiting to be made into quince jelly.*

Bramble jelly

Before starting, wash the blackberries (this is especially important if you pick blackberries from roadsides as the fruit may have a coating of grime), then soak for a few minutes in a solution of white vinegar and cold water. Rinse well.

450g (1lb) ripe blackberries
175ml (6fl oz) water
450g (1lb) granulated sugar
Juice of 1 lemon

Put the blackberries in a preserving pan with the water, stew gently with lid on for about 25 minutes. Stir and mash, then add the sugar and lemon juice. Continue cooking on a low heat until the sugar has completely dissolved. Working quickly, put the mush into a sieve lined with gauze and swiftly squeeze the jelly through. This jam sets very quickly – if it seems to be setting before it has passed through the sieve, just re-heat to melt it and continue putting it through the sieve. Pour into sterilized jars (see page 135).

Quince jelly

Quince, once known as 'marmelo' in Portuguese, used to be the main ingredient in marmalade. Quinces were not replaced by oranges until the nineteenth century.

900g (2lb) quinces, peeled, cored and sliced
(prepared weight)
900ml (1½ pints) water
Juice of 1 lemon
Sugar

Place the quinces in a preserving pan, add the water and simmer gently until tender and mushy. Add the sugar and stir until dissolved, boil until setting point has been reached (see page 135). Pot as normal.

Blackcurrant juice

This recipe produces a juice that is a million miles away from commercially made blackcurrant juice.

1.8kg (4lb) ripe blackcurrants
600ml (1 pint) cold water
1.8kg (4lb) sugar

Sometimes when I am short of time or am simply too lazy to pick through the fruit, I put the whole lot, leaves, stalks and all into the pan, add the water and the sugar and boil. As soon as the fruit is soft and dispersed and the sugar has melted, put the mush into a sieve lined with gauze and push the fruit through. The result is a thick, luscious cordial, which, when diluted with sparkling water, makes a delicious, sharp, refreshing drink.

Raspberry and herb cordial

To make the ice cubes, simply place a small herb sprig in each compartment of an ice-cube tray, cover with water and freeze.

1kg (2¼ lb) raspberries
Juice of 1 lemon, or more to taste
450g (1lb) sugar, or to taste
Ice cubes made with a sprig of herb (rosemary, hyssop, mint)

Carefully pick over the raspberries and place in a preserving pan. Slowly bring to the boil, stirring all the time until the fruit has given up its juice. Pour into a sieve lined with gauze and press the juice through. Return the juice to the pan and add the lemon juice and sugar, stir over a low heat until the sugar has dissolved. Decant into dry sterilized bottles (see page 134) and store in the refrigerator until required. Serve cold with sparkling water and herb ice cubes.

LEFT: *Home-made cordials, using the fruits of your labour.*

RIGHT: *Sloe gin makes a lovely gift – pick sloes after mid October for the best flavour.*

BELOW: *Freeze sprigs of herbs with water in ice-cube trays to flavour and chill drinks on hot summer days.*

Blackberry cordial

Put the cleaned and de-stalked fruits in a bowl and cover with two parts water and one part white wine vinegar. Leave in a cool place for two or three days. Strain the blackberries and place in a saucepan along with 450g (1lb) of sugar to every 450g (1lb) of fruit. Boil until the fruit is melted and the sugar dissolved. Strain through muslin laid in a sieve and bottle – the blackberry cordial will keep for several weeks in the refrigerator.

Sloe gin

Never having made sloe gin, I was struck by the beauty of a heavy crop of sloes growing in my garden. In my new regime of using the bounty on my doorstep I was moved to turn the dark, plum-coloured berries into Christmas gifts. The recipe is simple and the results delicious, even after only a day when really it is supposed to 'brew' for at least three months.

1.5kg (3¼lb) sloes
4 x 500ml bottles of gin
175g (6oz) fine sugar or to taste – I added a lot more, but then I have an extremely sweet tooth

If you have the patience and the recipients have the delicate palate to notice, prick each sloe with a needle to release the flavour.

Sterilize large glass jars (see page 134). I like to use either Le Parfait sealed jars (see page 132) or a collection of beautiful antique bottles with openings large enough to put the sloes into. Divide the sloes between the bottles, pour in the sugar and fill with gin. Remember to leave enough space for the contents to be shaken periodically. Seal the bottles and leave to brew for three months.

You are supposed to decant the contents, but personally I think that the sloes left inside the bottle look rather beautiful.

Apple relish

This is a good recipe to make in autumn as it uses up any unripe green tomatoes and windfall cooking apples.

1.8kg (4lb) green tomatoes
1 teaspoon salt
450g (1lb) cooking apples
550g (1¼lb) shallots
450g (1lb) red tomatoes
2 red peppers
450g (1lb) brown sugar
300ml (10fl oz) cider vinegar

Slice the green tomatoes thinly and sprinkle with salt. Leave for an hour or two. Peel, core and chop the apples and the shallots. Slice and remove the hard core of the red tomatoes. Put the peppers under the grill or in the oven to make removing the skin easier. Discard the core and seeds, then peel and chop. Rinse the green tomato slices and shake dry in a sieve. Put all ingredients, except the peppers and the red tomatoes, into a preserving pan and bring to the boil. Simmer for 20 minutes or until the liquid has evaporated. Add the peppers and red tomatoes. Simmer until thick. Pour into sterilized jars (see page 135).

Oven-dried tomatoes

Halve the tomatoes and scoop out the seeds. Make a paste with minced garlic, basil leaves, extra-virgin olive oil, freshly ground black pepper and sea salt and spread the mixture onto the tomato shells. Place in a shallow baking dish and leave in a low oven or the bottom oven of the Aga for 2–3 hours.

Herb oils and vinegars

The recipe works for both herb vinegars and oils. Use white wine vinegar as it is light and will absorb the flavour of the herb's own oil well. All fresh culinary herbs can be used. Feed sprigs of fresh herbs through the neck of the bottle of vinegar or oil. Seal and store in a cool dark place for up to two weeks before straining, labelling and re-bottling in clean bottles.

RIGHT: *Infuse oils and vinegars with herbs. For special gifts, tie a bundle of the dried herb to the bottle. Remove the herbs after a week of infusing and decant into sterilized bottles.*

BELOW: *Green tomatoes and red peppers add extra flavours to apple relish.*

CHAPTER 5

THE USEFULNESS OF HERBS

Since the life-changing discovery of antibiotics,
we have grown to expect quick solutions to our
problems. We are demanding antibiotics from our
doctors for instant cures for minor ailments that, given
time and a strong constitution and the help of something
as simple as, for example, garlic, would not only have
cured the ailment, but also created a more resistant
body with its own home-grown antibodies to deal with
the next bout of infection. According to investigations
carried out in 2007, 50 million of the 150 million
prescriptions written outside hospitals
are thought to be unnecessary.

Medicinal herbs

Used to treat various ailments since the beginning of time, herbs and flowers are often the basis for modern-day pharmaceutical drugs. Like our ancestors, we discover their benefits by trial and error in scientific research. Two medicinal plants that immediately spring to mind are the yew tree whose toxic berries are a vital part of tamoxifen, an oestrogen inhibitor used in the treatment or prevention of cancer, and the evening primrose flower, which has many applications in hormonal medicine.

Ancient remedies

For hundreds of years, apothecaries, housewives and herbalists worked in the 'still room', concocting tonics, poultices and lotions from leaves, flowers and roots. These were the only medicinal resources available to them for treating and curing illnesses.

During early medieval times the word 'herb' described all useful plants, which included vegetables as well as herbs as we know them today. It was not until the eighteenth century that herbs were given their own category, distinguishing their medicinal and life-enhancing properties from food plants. Alongside vegetable gardens, infirmary gardens were cultivated to grow specific herbs for the apothecary.

The history of a herb can often be deduced from its name. For instance, the names bishopswort, blind man's hand, fairy's thimbles and friar's cap all tell the tale of their ancient uses. At one time it was thought that the appearance of a plant indicated the part of the body it would heal. Its growing conditions, scent or special habits provided more clues.

Adam and Eve, also known as Lungwort (*Pulmonaria officinalis*) bore a close resemblance to a diseased lung and was thought to benefit lung conditions, and is in fact an effective expectorant. All Heal (*Prunella vulgaris*) earned its place among healing remedies because the upper lip of the flower resembled a hook, which was the main agricultural tool at the time of its discovery in the sixteenth century. Wounds caused by careless use of billhooks and sickles were treated to good effect with All Heal.

BE SAFE – SEEK EXPERT GUIDANCE

Herbal medicines can be as powerful as their chemical counterparts prescribed by doctors, so it is absolutely vital that before treating any ailment you SEEK THE ADVICE OF A QUALIFIED HERBAL PRACTITIONER. Synergism – which is the effect caused by combining more than one herbal remedy – can enhance the effect or can make it extremely dangerous. This is another reason why you should always take advice.

Other than as flavouring in cooking, herbs should never be taken during pregnancy or by children under 5 years old.

BELOW: *A wide selection
of herbs can be grown in
a small container, such as
this wooden wine box.*

Sensible use of herbal remedies

As I write, the debate has opened again about the efficacy (or not) of herbal remedies and the qualifications of herbal practitioners. The law on selling herbal remedies that claim to cure ailments is a little cloudy and, as far as I know, the rigorous testing required to license a chemical drug is not applied to herbal alternatives. Be cautious when self-administering herbal preparations, and always confirm your suspicions about ailments with your doctor. Self-diagnosis is fine for minor complaints, but these can be the start of something more serious. Be aware of your body, and any changes you experience, and confirm with your doctor that the herbal preparations you want to take are suitable.

Protecting wild herbs

Interest in herbal medicine is increasing. The more knowledgeable and informed we become about the side effects of conventional medicine, the more we seek alternative remedies – homeopathic, flower and herbal. This renewed interest has a downside, though. It was always believed that herbs gathered from the wild were more efficacious than cultivated plants, and 90 per cent of all herbs used in medicine today are still gathered from the wild. According to the Vegan Society, the herb goldenseal (*Hydrastis canadensis*), used for immune deficiency problems, is now listed by CITES (Convention of Trade in Endangered Species) as the fifth most endangered plant species on the planet. When buying herbal tinctures and preparations, check that all ingredients come from sustainable sources, and that a registered, ecologically-sound company manufactures the product.

Growing herbs

The best option is to grow your own herbs and, with the advice and help of your practitioner, make your own remedies. If you find that a specific herb eases symptoms or guards against your particular weaknesses, make sure you have your own sustainable supply. Herbs make beautiful and useful growing companions for flowers, fruit and vegetables, and in the section on companion planting (see pages 114–115) you will see that their strong scents can not only act as deterrents to pests but also encourage those creatures most likely to feed on any that do persist.

Popular medicinal herbs

The following list includes herbs that are commonly grown or easily found. I stress again that, unless you are using herbs to flavour food and drinks, seek advice from a herbal practitioner. Never rely solely on home treatment for any medical complaint. Where appropriate, I have suggested cures for animals, but take advice from your veterinary practitioner before use.

Aloe Vera

This grows wild in arid areas of Europe, America and Africa. It will not tolerate frost, but can be cultivated as an indoor plant in more northerly regions. Personally, I find it ugly in the extreme, but its healing powers are very effective in the treatment of sunburn and minor burns. The gel extruded when the leaves are cut can be applied to all sorts of wounds. It forms a protective layer, encouraging skin regeneration. When ingested, aloe vera is thought to be an effective intestinal cleanser. In this case, it is best to buy ready-made preparations from a reputable source. Aloe vera is also used in hand creams and shampoo.

Aaron's Rod (*Verbascum thapsus*)

Also known as goldenrod, this grows widely in Europe and North America. It is used to treat urinary tract and kidney infections, and also to ease catarrh. Gather the flowering tops of the plant in summer and dry them. They can be made into a cold compress to use as an anti-inflammatory dressing for wounds and stings, or into a calming tea.

All Heal (*Prunella vulgaris*)

This plant, also known as self-heal, woundwort or sticklewort, grows wild throughout temperate regions of the world, and is easy to establish. All Heal is useful for treating sore throats and inflammations of the mouth, but its history is rich and varied. It has been used to treat ailments from quinsy to diphtheria, and wounds caused by careless handling of farming tools.

Basil (*Ocimum basilicum*)

The name of this popular herb is derived from the Greek *Basilikon photon*, which translates as 'kingly herb'. However, basil has a mixed, rather than royal, history – adorning altars in some Greek Orthodox churches, it has also been denounced as a plant of the devil. Cultivated for over 2,000 years, it originates in India, and was introduced to Mediterranean countries via the spice routes. Its medicinal uses are limited but its oil is said to combat mental fatigue, and vinegar flavoured by its leaves can be added to bath water as an antiseptic. Its main use, however, is in salads and cooking. The leaves aid digestion as well as adding exotic flavour. The juice of basil leaves rubbed on skin acts as an insect repellent.

BELOW: *The bright green leaves of basil.*

Celery *(Apium graveolens)*

Although more commonly known as a salad vegetable, celery stems have a calming effect on the gut and are helpful in the detoxification of the kidneys. Eaten raw, celery has a beneficial effect on arthritis.

Chamomile *(Matricaria chamomilla)*

A lovely, low-growing plant, chamomile resembles a daisy. Collect and dry the flowers from June to August. Chamomile is commonly used for its sedative properties, but it also relieves morning sickness, haemorrhoids, mastitis, eczema and hayfever. When planted in close proximity to ailing plants, chamomile is reputed to help in their recovery.

Cinnamon *(Cinnamomum zeylanicum)*

A spice rather than a herb, cinnamon comes from the bark of the *Cinnamomum verum* tree, native to Sri Lanka and southern India. Its strong flavour is due to the essential oil that makes up one per cent of its composition. Principally employed in cooking, cinnamon is also used as an insect repellent, to ease the symptoms of colds, and to aid digestive problems, but use it sparingly.

Cloves *(Syzgium aromaticum)*

Cloves are also a spice rather than a herb. They have extraordinary healing and pain-relieving powers, and medicinally no other substance has been found to equal their efficacy in relieving toothache. They are also used as a local antiseptic. Lesser known is the effect of cloves on relieving nausea – two drops of the essential oil in water are said to stop vomiting. Cloves stuck into an orange are traditionally used to repel moths.

Coriander *(Coriandrum sativum)*

A native of southern Europe and the Middle East, coriander was brought to northern Europe

HERB TEAS

Both medicinally and for pure pleasure, fresh or dried herbs make a gentle and refreshing alternative to normal teas. Mix with fresh orange or lemon peel for added flavour, and sweeten with honey if desired. Use one teaspoon for each cup of boiling water, and leave to steep for five minutes.

The following herbs all make delicious teas: basil, caraway, chamomile, elderflower (use only the flowers), fennel, fenugreek, hibiscus, hyssop, lavender (use both the leaves and the flowers), lemon balm, lemon verbena, mint, raspberry leaf, rose petal, rosemary, sage, thyme.

by the Romans, who used it with cumin and vinegar as a preservative. Easily grown from seed in light, well-drained soil, coriander thrives in a sunny position and has many culinary uses. Medicinally, coriander leaves aid digestion, reduce flatulence and stimulate appetite. The dried seeds can be applied in a poultice to relieve painful joints.

Dandelion *(Taraxacum officinale)*

This has many uses and all of the plant is safe to use. The young leaves, collected before the flowers appear, are good in salads, contain more iron and calcium than spinach and are rich in vitamins A and C. The leaves are a powerful diuretic, and can be boiled with honey to treat coughs. Dandelions are regarded as one of the best remedies for liver and kidney complaints. The dried roots, dug up in autumn, can be used as a coffee substitute, which acts as a diuretic and is said to cleanse the liver; they are also a mild laxative, and a tonic made from them treats constipation and dyspepsia. The milk from cut flower stems is a mosquito repellent and is said to cure warts. Steeped in boiling water and cooled, dandelions can be used to fertilize plants as they contain a good supply of copper.

ABOVE: *Not just a garden weed, dandelion has many uses.*

Dill *(Anethum graveolens)*

Remains of this plant have been found in the ruins of Roman buildings in Britain, and it is mentioned in Egyptian herbals dating back more than 5,000 years. Dill is said to improve the appetite and aid digestion. Chewing the small seeds prevents halitosis, and the crushed seed heads steeped in hot water make a nail-strengthening bath.

Elder *(Sambucus nigra)*

Elder flowers, used to make elderflower cordial, are beneficial in alleviating catarrh and respiratory complaints. A compress made from the flowers steeped in hot water can be used to ease conjunctivitis as well as chilblains. A gargle made from an elderflower infusion can soothe sore throats. The flowers can also be infused in vinegar and used in the same way.

Unless cooked, elderberries are *not* to be eaten under any circumstances; even the juice must not be swallowed unless it has been boiled. To make a cure for toothache and migraines, boil the elderberries with a small amount of water, then push the mush through a sieve lined with fine gauze. Measure the juice and return it to the pan, adding 450g (1lb) of sugar for each 600ml (1 pint) of juice. Boil, stirring, until the mixture reaches a jam consistency. Bottle in sterilized jars and keep refrigerated until needed. Take two teaspoons when required.

BELOW: *Growing herbs in windowboxes allows urban dwellers an accessible supply of fresh herbs.*

ABOVE: *The feathery fronds of fennel.*

Fennel *(Foeniculum vulgare)*

All parts of the fennel plant are used – the leaves, the seed and the bulb. As a digestive aid, fennel has been used since the ancient Greeks discovered that it stilled a hungry tummy, and I am delighted to have stumbled upon this as a natural slimming aid. Fennel seeds steeped in water make an aid to digestion, heartburn and constipation, and a teaspoon of cooled fennel tea comforts babies suffering from colic.

WARNING: fennel essence taken in large doses has been known to cause convulsions and disturb the nervous system.

Feverfew *(Tanacetum parthenium)*

As its name suggests, feverfew was probably used to heal fevers. After extensive clinical trials during the 1970s, it was proven to reduce migraines both in intensity and frequency. The leaves have a very bitter taste – sandwiching two or three small leaves between two slices of bread helps to disguise it. Consult a medical practitioner before taking feverfew as it is not suitable for everyone, and do not take more than the recommended dose as this can cause unpleasant side effects. Easily grown, once established feverfew will self-seed.

LEFT: *The daisy-like flowers of feverfew.*

Garlic *(Allium sativum)*

Garlic is such a powerful plant that some risks are associated with it. It is important to remember that with all herbs valued for their medicinal properties, something that benefits one person may be harmful to another.

Botulism *(clostridium botulinum)* presents the most serious risk associated with garlic. The bulb's sulphurous nature makes garlic a breeding ground for this dangerous toxin, which can cause major, sometimes fatal, stomach illness. The danger arises if raw garlic is stored in oil at room temperature or for too long in the refrigerator, so never store raw garlic in this way. When making salad dressings, don't leave it for too long before use. As a rough guide, garlic in oil can be stored for up to two weeks in the refrigerator. Fresh cloves can be kept at room temperature for up to a month. It is obvious when garlic is past its prime – it will become soft, its pungency will have weakened and a green shoot may be visible.

Garlic can interfere with certain prescription medicines, especially some anti-coagulants used in surgery. In addition, research has concluded that garlic supplements 'can cause a potentially harmful side effect when combined with a type of medication used to treat HIV/AIDS'.

However, garlic is praised for its cardiovascular benefits and its ability to reduce cholesterol and ward off germs. Because of its strength and power (and raw garlic is more potent than cooked garlic) use it wisely, gauge its effects, and do not over-indulge.

Herb of St John *(Hypericum perforatum)*

Also known as St John's Wort, the yellow flowers of this herb were once believed to cure cases of mania. It is still used to alleviate depression but dependence upon drugs made from this herb has been known and it should be administered only

RIGHT: *A traditional plait of garlic bulbs.*

by a qualified practitioner. Stopping treatment must be done under supervision.

Externally, the oil extracted from the flowers may be applied to ease neuralgia, varicose veins and ulcers. It also relieves sunburn.

To grow herb of St John, sow seeds in the spring where you want the plant to flower – it is very hardy and spreads easily by self-seeding, so keep cutting back to avoid it taking over.

Horseradish (*Armoracia rusticana*)

Both roots and leaves of the horseradish plant are used in cooking. The well-known sauce is made by grating the fresh root, and the young leaves picked in spring can be used in salads. Chopped finely, you can add them to dog and cat food to dispel worms. Horseradish has strong antibiotic properties, and is good for restoring poor circulation. It is also sometimes used as a diuretic for urinary infections, and to relieve rheumatism and gout. A poultice made from fresh grated roots and applied to chilblains or stiff joints and muscles will alleviate discomfort, and is also believed to relieve backache. Over-use of horseradish may cause blisters. Do not use if your thyroid function is low or if thyroxin has been prescribed. Use sparingly if pregnant or suffering from kidney problems.

Hyssop (*Hyssopus officinalis*)

As well as being a delicious addition to a green salad and Pimms cocktails, hyssop leaves may be used in infusions to alleviate coughs and asthma or complaints of the upper respiratory tract. Externally, it can be used for bruises and burns and/was once used as a remedy for rheumatism.

Although hyssop is safe if used professionally and with care, it should not be used on anyone with nervous irritability. Its distilled oil is not suitable in aromatherapy on patients with a highly strung disposition as it is capable of causing epileptic fits. Hyssop should never be taken in pregnancy, even in salads or beverages.

Jacob's Ladder (*Polemonium caeruleum*)

This beautiful plant can be propagated from seed or by dividing the plant just after the stalks die down in the autumn. Medicinally, the powdered roots and rhizomes can be made into a poultice for bruises, inflammation and wounds, and the herb is good for dealing with skin blemishes when used as a face wash or for counteracting the effects of poison ivy. Taken internally, the plant is poisonous in its entirety, and to be used only when directed by a qualified herbal practitioner.

Kiss Me Quick (*Gallium odoratum*)

Sweet woodruff, as this herb is also known, was once used to scent linen and stuff mattresses. Medicinally, it is made into a tea that is said to relieve stomach pain. It also acts as a diuretic and is thought to help relieve gall stones.

A hardy perennial, this herb has pretty, star-shaped flowers which can be used sparingly in salads. It can be grown in pots, but quickly becomes root bound. Consumption of large quantities can produce symptoms of poisoning, including dizziness and vomiting, so use with care.

Lady's Mantle (*Alchemilla mollis*)

This is also known as Silvery Lady's Mantle. A beautiful plant with green, lobed leaves and greenish-yellow flowers in summer, it thrives and self-seeds in most soils (even in dry gravel and stone walls) but does not do well in wet or boggy ground. The very young leaves can be used in salads. They are slightly bitter but mild in taste.

It is traditionally used for menstrual disorders, and as a mouthwash after a tooth extraction. It can be used to treat diarrhoea in pets.

Lavender (*Lavandula angustifolia*)

Growing well in many climes, lavender requires a warm, sunny aspect and well-drained soil, but is as happy in pots as it is in the ground. The flowers deter flies and moths and the oil made from the leaves has a beneficial effect on stings, burns, cuts and grazes. Lavender oil has strong antibacterial properties and kills the diphtheria and typhoid bacilli, as well as streptococcus and pneumococcus. Adding the oil to a warm bath helps to assuage depression and anxiety and relieves headaches. Pour a few drops of lavender oil into bath water to ensure a good night's sleep, or to calm an irritable child.

Lemon Balm *(Melissa officinalis)*
Also known as balm mint, lemon balm is widely grown in Europe and North America, often near orchards to attract bees. Its medicinal properties include relief from headaches and nervous disorders, such as tension and memory loss. A tea made from the fresh leaves of lemon balm aids digestion, colic and flatulence. Lemon balm oil is used in aromatherapy to treat depression and sleeplessness. It is a good idea to grow lemon balm in a pot because, like common mint, the roots are very invasive.

Liquorice *(Liquiritia officinalis)*
Used medicinally for over 3,000 years, liquorice was first discovered by the Greeks. These days it is grown in Russia, Spain, India and throughout the temperate zones of the world. It became an important crop, used to disguise the unpleasant taste of other medicines while providing a soothing juice to alleviate troublesome coughs.

The dried root, which is stripped of its outer, bitter bark, is used as a remedy for colds, sore throats and bronchial catarrh. As a gentle remedy for constipation, it also lowers the level of stomach acid and relieves heartburn. Liquorice juice is beneficial in healing stomach ulcers, coating the stomach wall and easing spasms of the large intestine. It is also thought to reduce levels of cholesterol in the blood.

RIGHT: *Lavender, ever-popular due to its flowers and scent.*

Marigold (Calendula officinalis)

This annual herb thrives in most climes and was first used in Indian and Arabic cultures. Known for its antiseptic, anti-fungal and anti-bacterial properties, it is used in the preparation of calendula cream – a homeopathic remedy effective in treating burns, grazes, scalds and stings. It is also used in the treatment of varicose veins, chilblains and impetigo. The petals steeped in boiling water and cooled make an eyewash for the treatment of conjunctivitis, and can be used to relieve the symptoms of thrush. The sap from the stem is said to cure warts, corns and calluses.

Marjoram (Origanum majorana)

This flowering plant has many species to its name. Also known as oregano in Mediterranean countries, this herb grows wild as well as being cultivated in pots or beds. The Romans and Greeks used its oils as a disinfectant and as a preservative. Medicinally, it is still used as an antiseptic owing to its high thymol content. Marjoram tea is a comfort to those suffering from bad colds, and has a calming effect on nerves as well as helping to settle an upset stomach and relieve sea sickness. Like chamomile, marjoram is helpful in aiding restful sleep when a few drops of the essential oil are dripped onto a handkerchief and laid on a pillow. Fresh marjoram leaves rubbed on gums will soothe the pain of toothache.

Nasturtium (Tropaeolum majus)

Also known as Indian cress, this self-seeding and prolific plant is grown worldwide. The deep orange and yellow flowers, which are rich in iron and vitamin C, may be used fresh in salads and as a pretty decoration on puddings and ice creams. To make a tea, steep the peppery-flavoured flowers in boiling water. The flower buds can be pickled in vinegar and used as an alternative to capers.

Nettle (Urtica dioica)

This seemingly spiteful plant grows prolifically in fertile soil. Use the young spring leaves as a vegetable, cooking them before eating – they are rich in vitamins and minerals. Nettles are beneficial in treating internal haemorrhages and haemorrhoids, and have a laxative effect. Made into a tonic, nettles can be used to treat eczema and anaemia, providing the right minerals. Their vitamin C content ensures that the minerals are fully absorbed.

Nettles can also be used as an insecticide. Fill a bucket full of nettles, cover with rainwater and steep for a week. Use the liquid in a spray bottle to rid your plants of blackfly and aphids.

Onion (Allium cepa)

Onions of any sort are key ingredients in making a natural cough syrup. Slice the onions and lay them flat in a shallow bowl, drizzle with honey and cover; leave to infuse for two to three hours and drain off the resulting liquid. Administer the syrup by teaspoon to relieve coughs and a tight chest.

BELOW: *Cough syrup prepared from onions and honey.*

Onion flower *(Allium ursinum)*

Also know as wild garlic, this grows profusely in Europe, Asia and many countries in the northern hemisphere. The fresh young leaves are delicious in salads and can also be made into soups. Wild garlic has been shown to reduce blood pressure, and is therefore beneficial in preventing strokes. It is also used to ease diarrhoea and dysentery, tuberculosis, whooping cough, typhoid and hepatitis, not to mention its beneficial effects in expelling worms. Effective in reducing blood sugar levels, wild garlic can help to control diabetes.

Herbal practitioners use wild garlic to treat toothache, earache, coughs, colds, insect bites and boils. It is also traditionally used to make a household disinfectant.

Parsley *(Petroselinum crispum)*

Traditionally used to treat bad breath as the result of eating garlic, the parsley plant is also rich in vitamin C, minerals and the antiseptic chlorophyll. It can help in relieving urinary infections and, in poultices, acts as an antiseptic dressing for wounds, sprains and insect bites.

Parsley freezes well and can be used straight from the freezer. Instead of chopping the leaves, it can simply be crumbled in its frozen state.

Peppermint *(Mentha piperita)*

The leaves of this useful plant are aromatic, antiseptic, antispasmodic, antibacterial and anti-parasitic. The torn leaves steeped in boiling water make a refreshing drink, served either hot or cold with ice. Hot mint tea can relieve headaches and increase ability to concentrate. Mint is helpful in relieving gastro-intestinal disorders, and is an appetite stimulant. It is best to grow mint in pots, because its roots are extremely invasive.

Raspberry leaves

Tea made from dried raspberry leaves is a good cure for diarrhoea. Gargle with the tea to soothe a sore throat.

ABOVE: *Rosemary, a herb widely used in cooking.*

Rosemary *(Rosmarinus officinalis)*

Steeped in myth and magical tales, rosemary was often used to purify the air in the sickroom. Rosemary oil is a very powerful agent and must be used with care and never taken internally. Externally, the oil has antibacterial properties and is said to ease headaches, improve circulation and deter insects. Infuse the fresh leaves in boiling water to make a mouthwash for sweet-smelling breath. Taken in small amounts, this infusion also reduces flatulence. Its antibacterial properties make it a good addition to bath water for healthy skin.

A useful companion plant (see pages 114–115), when grown near carrots, rosemary will repel carrot fly, and it is generally beneficial to sage when planted close by.

ABOVE: *The leaves of Russian comfrey.*

Russian Comfrey *(Symphytum officinale)*
Also known as Saracen's root. Mainly used in poultices to heal wounds and reduce bruising, comfrey is also used in the treatment of athlete's foot and mastitis. Its leaves contain allantoin, an agent that stimulates healthy tissue formation, which probably explains why it is often used in the manufacture of skin-softening cosmetics.

Sage *(Salvia officinalis)*
Medicinally, this plant is highly regarded. Also known as salvia from the Latin *salveo*, meaning 'I save', it is used to treat colds and, when made into a tisane with a little cider vinegar, is effective as a gargle to treat sore throat, laryngitis and tonsillitis. The mouthwash may also be used to treat mouth ulcers and infections of the gums.

Thyme *(Thymus spp.)*
Although thyme grows prolifically in the wild, it can be cultivated in pots and in herb gardens. There are hundreds of species and many of them prefer poor, free-draining soil. The tiny leaves give off a pungent, heady scent in the heat. Used in cooking, the oils break down fatty foods, particularly in oily fish dishes and stews. Thyme has strong antiseptic properties and the essential oil, which is toxic and must never be ingested, is also antibacterial and anti-fungal. A few drops used in bath water is said to relieve the pain of rheumatism. Avoid completely if pregnant.

Vervain *(Verbena officinalis)*
Said to have been used to stem the flow of Christ's blood at the crucifixion, vervain is also known as holy herb. Vervain has been used to ease nervous exhaustion and depression for hundreds of years, and is now also used in the treatment of liver problems and urinary tract infections.

Sweet Violet *(Viola odorata)*
Sweet violet flowers are used extensively in the making of perfume, and are also crystallized and used for culinary purposes. Various parts of the plant are used medicinally. The rootstock is made into a soothing expectorant, used to treat respiratory disorders such as bronchitis, coughs and head colds. Made into a poultice, the leaves soothe sore nipples. The crystallized flowers have a reputation for aiding sleep.

Woodbine *(Lonicera periclymenum)*
Common all over Europe, northern Africa and North America, woodbine is more usually known by its alternative name, honeysuckle. Tea made from its perfumed flowers soothes coughs and asthma. Research has also proved that this tea can be helpful in soothing the pain of colitis. The raw flowers can be used sparingly in salads.

Yarrow *(Achillea millefolium)*
Creeping rootstock ensures that yarrow, also known as woundwort, survives whatever situation it may find itself in, and it is common all over the world, usually on waste ground. Medicinally, it is one of the best-known remedies for curing fevers. Used as an infusion, it induces sweats that cool fevers and expel toxins. The Chinese use it in a poultice for healing wounds.

Yarrow also encourages speedy decomposition of waste vegetation, making it an essential, albeit not very beautiful, addition to the organic garden.

bouquet garni herbs

Little muslin bags of bouquet garni seem to have all but disappeared from our lives. If using straight away, fresh herbs are more potent, but dried keep longer. A selection specially prepared to suit different foods, presented in a box, makes a lovely gift. Add your own favourite recipes using each one to make it even more special.

you will need
Selection of herbs
String
Muslin
Ribbon
Decorative box
Tissue paper

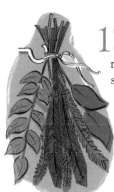

1 Gather a selection of herbs, tie them round the stems in small bunches and hang up to dry.

2 Cut some muslin squares, about 20 x 20cm (8 x 8in).

3 Place some dried herbs on each muslin square – use the list below for guidance.
For chicken: chives, thyme and rosemary
For game: juniper berries, rosemary and bay leaves
For lamb: rosemary or lemon thyme and parsley
For beef: thyme with lemon thyme or bay
For pork: rosemary or sage with parsley
For tomato dishes: oregano, parsley and chives
For potatoes: sage with bay or thyme

4 Gather each muslin square at the corners and tie with ribbon or string.

5 Put them in a decorative box, lined with tissue paper.

Home-made medicinal preparations

For minor complaints such as sunburn or for practical alternatives to products such as insect repellent, it is safe to make your own preparations.

Sage lotion for sunburned skin

Tear a handful of fresh sage leaves into a bowl, cover with boiling water and infuse for 20 minutes. Strain into a bottle, keep in the fridge and apply when needed.

St John's Wort lotion

The mashed yellow flowers of St John's Wort mixed with olive oil make a soothing lotion for sunburn or varicose veins.

Peppermint oil for muscular pain

To relieve sore muscles, massage the affected area with peppermint oil. If you use a commercial preparation, check it is suitable for external use.

Basil mosquito repellent

Simply crush basil leaves and rub them onto areas of exposed skin to repel mosquitoes.

Disinfect with feverfew

To disinfect slight wounds and to aid restful sleep, gather dried or fresh feverfew flowers in muslin bath bags (see page 163) and add to bath water.

Removing nits from hair

Soak your hair in neat white distilled vinegar, wrap it in a towel for an hour, then comb with a nit comb to remove the creatures before washing your hair again. Finish with another coating of vinegar without rinsing off – this leaves hair glossy and shiny. Combing neat vodka through hair also removes nits.

Combat hair loss

Drink a banana smoothie made from mashed bananas, honey, yoghurt and low-fat milk regularly as this mixture is rich in biotin, which is said to prevent hair loss.

MEDICINAL USES FOR WHITE DISTILLED VINEGAR

Bee stings To soothe bee stings hold a cotton pad soaked in vinegar on the affected part.

Blocked sinuses Make a vaporizer by adding a quarter cup of vinegar to steaming water and inhale the fumes to help clear sinuses.

Burns Keep a container of vinegar in the fridge and apply to minor burns to relieve pain.

Sunburn To soothe sunburn, apply vinegar with a soft pad of cotton.

Dandruff To rid the scalp of dandruff, use a solution of half a cup of vinegar and two cups of warm water.

Sore throats To soothe a sore throat, gargle with a glass of water to which you have added two tablespoons of vinegar.

Hot toddies If you don't have a lemon to add to a hot toddy for soothing a cold, use vinegar and honey in hot water.

cucumber lotion

Home-grown, organic cucumber makes a deliciously cool lotion, especially for the face, marvellous for hot summer days. It's also very soothing when applied to sunburned skin. Keep a bottle of the lotion in the fridge, and use within two weeks.

you will need

Fresh cucumber
Sieve
Fine muslin
Glass jar or spray bottle
Eau de cologne

1 Coarsely grate a firm, fresh cucumber and place in a sieve lined with fine muslin.

2 Place the sieve over a bowl and push the cucumber through the muslin to release the juice.

3 Pour the resulting liquid into a clean glass jar or spray bottle.

4 Add a few drops of eau de cologne for a scented lotion, and apply as required.

Home-made beauty preparations

You will find that your store-cupboard essentials (see pages 120–121) are not just useful in the kitchen, but in the bathroom as well. Many bath and beauty preparations will benefit from the addition of fresh or dried herbs.

For the bath

Making your own bath preparations is extremely simple, will save you a great deal of money and ensure that you are bathing in the purest of ingredients.

Basic body scrub

Smooth, blemish-free skin is easily achieved with the help of just a few basic ingredients. You can be sure that home-made scrubs are pure, with no added chemicals, and can be custom made to suit all types of skin.

225g (8oz) sea salt crystals
4 tablespoons olive oil
juice of 1 lemon or lime

Mix all the ingredients together and rub all over the body once a week to exfoliate skin, concentrating on problem areas, such as knees, feet and elbows, then shower off. The lime or lemon juice in the mixture acts as a bleaching agent that will whiten your finger- and toenails. The scrub can also be used as a cuticle softener, both on feet and hands.

For extra therapeutic benefits, add some fresh or dried herbs to your body scrub. My suggestions are:

- comfrey, for rejuvenation and softening of the skin
- lavender flowers, to promote restful sleep
- elderflowers steeped in water, to whiten and soften the skin, and to lighten freckles
- mint, for a fresh and invigorating sense of well being
- rosemary, to invigorate and energize
- vervain, to alleviate nervous exhaustion
- thyme, for its antibacterial properties

Refreshing morning bath tonic

For an extremely invigorating tonic, add crushed wormwood leaves to cider vinegar and leave to infuse. Store in a glass jar with a non-metallic lid. Add this to running bath water in the morning for a fresh start to the day.

Bath teas

Infuse fresh bay leaves in boiling water and add the strained bay tea to a hot bath to relieve aching limbs. For healthy skin, pour a cup of strong rosemary tea into bath water.

Deep cleanse with fennel

For really deep cleansing, use fennel seeds and leaves with porridge oats in your bath bag (see facing page for making instructions).

oatmeal bath bags

Organic porridge oats make a wonderful skin softener when added to bath water. Make a selection and, if you can bear to, give some away as presents but be sure to indulge yourself as well.

you will need
Muslin
Organic porridge oats
Herbs, either flowers or sprigs
Ribbon or string

1 Cut some squares of muslin measuring approximately 20 x 20cm (8 x 8in).

2 Place a handful of organic porridge oats together with some herb flowers, or a sprig or two of your chosen herb, on each square of muslin, gather up the corners and tie securely with ribbon or string to form a bag.

3 Make the ribbon long enough to tie to the hot-water tap so that the running water deluges the bag. Alternatively, just drop the bag in the bath, immersing it in the water, and squeeze it gently until the water turns milky soft.

LEFT AND BELOW: *Sea salt not only makes an excellent exfoliant, but also softens bath water. Fill jars with natural sea salt and add either olive oil or a scented oils. Lavender oil makes particularly beautiful bath salts and, if used at night, will promote restful sleep. Other herbs, oils and fresh or dried flowers can be added to make unique customized bath salts – try rosemary oil with a sprig of rosemary or rose oil with dried rosebuds. If using fresh herbs or flowers, use within one or two weeks, before the flower petals or leaves lose their colour.*

Hair and scalp

To improve the condition of your scalp and make your hair strong and shiny, experiment with the following herbal treatments.

Brightening fair hair

Steep the leaves of betony, also known as bishopswort, in hot water to make a yellow dye that will highlight light-coloured hair. Chamomile water in the final rinse is also good for fair hair – pour boiling water over fresh chamomile flowers, leave for an hour and use when cooled.

Adding shine to dark hair

Rosemary tea as a final rinse leaves dark hair shiny and glossy.

Nettle scalp tonic

Not only do nettles have a good reputation for encouraging hair growth but they eliminate dandruff. Boil a large rubber-gloved handful of nettles in water and simmer for 10 minutes, cool and strain the liquid. Store it in the fridge and use when required.

Horsetail hair tonic

A common and invasive weed, horsetail is very probably growing, uninvited, in your garden. Steep a bunch of horsetail in simmering water for 20 minutes. This decoction can be used as a tonic to strengthen your hair. After shampooing, rinse and pour a jugful of cooled horsetail water over your hair, wrap your head in a warm towel for 20 minutes before rinsing. The lotion can also be used as a nail strengthener.

Parsley seed hair tonic

Crush parsley seeds and steep them in water to make a hair rinse that will leave hair shiny and glossy. It is also said to eliminate head lice. Pour the rinse over your head and wrap in a towel for an hour. Do not rinse off and allow hair to dry naturally.

Malt vinegar hair tonic

To add a glowing shine to your hair, add half a cup of malt vinegar to the final rinse.

Dry shampoo

If you have no time to shampoo your hair before going out, dust it with talcum powder or corn flour and brush it out. Try this out first when you are not in a hurry to make sure that it works in the way you want.

BELOW: *Often found growing in the wild, nettles make a wonderful tonic for the scalp.*

Skin lotions and face packs

Here are some easy recipes for my favourite beautifying skin lotions and face packs.

Marsh mallow hand lotion

This is a wonderful lotion for dry, chapped hands.

28g (1oz) marsh mallow root
cold spring water
2 tablespoons ground almonds
1 teaspoon milk
1 teaspoon cider vinegar
lavender oil or olive oil

Chop the marsh mallow root finely and soak in cold spring water for 24 hours. Stir and strain well through a muslin-lined sieve. Add one tablespoon of the mallow juice to the ground almonds, milk and cider vinegar. Mix together with a few drops of lavender oil if you want a scented lotion; olive oil if you do not. Pour into a clean, dry, screw-top jar and keep in the fridge, using as required.

Chervil skin cleanser

This is a wonderful cleanser for keeping your skin supple and preventing wrinkles. Infuse a handful of fresh chervil leaves in boiling water and cool, then use the chervil water to cleanse the skin.

Honey and fennel face pack

A sticky face pack made with fennel and honey is said to prevent wrinkles. Chop a bulb of fennel, including the leaves, very finely. Mix with two tablespoons of solid honey and apply. Leave for 15–20 minutes, then wash off.

Tired eyes

To cool your eyes, make eye pads using thick slices of cucumber. Another option is to use cotton pads soaked in cold milk. Lie down, place the pads on closed eyes and relax for a while.

Borage facial

For a monthly deep facial clean, pour boiling water over a handful of borage leaves in a large bowl. Make a tent with a towel draped over your head and, keeping your eyes tightly closed, steam your face for 10 minutes. If it's too much for you, come up for air when necessary. Rinse your face with cool chervil water.

Strawberry face pack

The juice and flesh of fresh strawberries make a lovely face pack, and are said to whiten skin and lighten freckles. Mash the fruit and spread all over the face – lying down so that it doesn't slide off. After 20 minutes wash off the face pack – or eat it!

BELOW: *If you can resist eating them, strawberries make a great face pack.*

Epsom salts

Epsom salts were much used by our parents' generation in the garden (see pages 105–106). However, they have many beauty uses too. They contain magnesium sulphate, which is absorbed through the skin when added to bath water. This draws toxins from the body, soothes the nervous system, reduces swelling, relaxes tired muscles, is a natural emollient and also an excellent exfoliator.

Note: It is important to check with your doctor before using Epsom salts if you have any health concerns.

Bath soak

Add 2 cups of Epsom salts to your bath water for a relaxing and sleep-inducing bath.

Face cleanser

To clean your face at night, mix half a teaspoon of Epsom salts with your regular cleansing cream. Massage into the skin and rinse with cold water.

Skin exfoliator

Massage handfuls of Epsom salts over wet skin in the shower, starting with your feet and continuing up towards the face. Rinse off in warm water.

Foot soak

To soothe aches, remove odours, and soften rough skin, add half a cup of Epsom salts to a large bowl of warm water. Soak your feet for as long as you like, then rinse in warm water and dry thoroughly.

Sprains and bruises

Epsom salts will reduce the swelling caused by sprains and bruises. Add 2 cups to a warm bath and soak.

Removing splinters

Soaking the finger in a solution of Epsom salts will draw the splinter out.

AGE SPOT TREATMENT

To delay the appearance of age spots on your hands, or to lighten existing ones, rub a piece of lemon all over your hands before washing. You can also treat freckles in the same way.

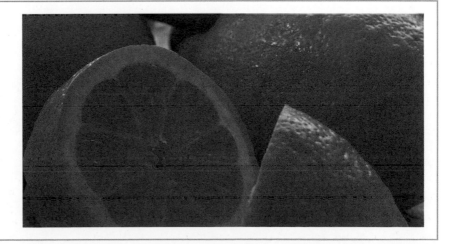

CHAPTER 6

INSPIRED GIFTS

During a visit to an outdoor antiques fair, it occurred to me that the atmosphere and bustle were so much more invigorating and pleasing than a crowded department store at Christmas time. Even though the likelihood of losing a possible purchase is far higher than it would be in a crowded shopping mall, the whole ritual of seeking and discovering extraordinary and unexpected treasures is pure pleasure. Could it be because the whole point about antiques is that they are recycled? Most are rare, some are unique, quite a lot are simply tat, but interesting tat – somebody once loved each and every object. This is probably the third or fourth time these objects have changed hands. they have all been pre-owned and pre-loved, and here they are again.

Antiques fairs

How likely is it that in 50 years' time the antiques markets of the day will be filled with game boys, plastic toys and flat-screened televisions? I don't think we will marvel at how beautifully these things were made. How heavenly would it be if, for just one season, everybody spent the time seeking out vintage gifts rather than new ones? Think of all the energy, pollution and air miles that could be saved. Not only that, but antiques are usually more beautifully made, could hold their value, or even become more valuable, over the years, and they are more likely to be unique.

As with most advice in this book, this involves more time. However, the time it takes to seek out antiques fairs and find the perfect gift is, in my experience, worth the effort. Start assembling Christmas and birthday presents in January and you might just be able to complete your list by November. What a pleasure to know that you will not have to fight the hysterical crowds in department stores and spend far more than you intended because you slid into panic-purchase mode.

Lasting enjoyment

This chapter on vintage/recycled/antique artefacts naturally encompasses finding original gifts, but I need no encouragement to furnish my home with antiques – it always has been and always will be a great pleasure. Apart from the obvious joy of buying antiquities, the fact that they have lasted many years and are still earning their keep generations later means that they were worth making in the first place. The sad fact behind our ever-increasing landfill sites is that the time, effort, design, manufacture and distribution of so much is disregarded so very easily.

A quote by Edmond de Goncourt, an eminent French collector, in an old book written by Barbara Milo Ohrbach, sums up the rules: 'If you ever take up collecting, each time you are tempted by a work of art, or by a curio, be sure to ask yourself before deciding to buy: can I live with it,

RIGHT: *An assortment of other people's cast-offs becomes exciting and enticing treasure in the atmosphere of an antiques market. The amazingly wide range of artefacts and tat ensures that there will be something for almost everyone.*

keep it in front of my eyes, and love it until I die?' We might feel this way for approximately one minute about a mass-produced frock, but do we really want to keep it in front of our eyes until we die – I don't think so. However, the tiny lambs (see right) would be very welcome to sit before my eyes until I die – they would be a great pleasure.

The most important thing to remember when buying second-hand goods, because that is what antiquities are, is to love them, not for their potential value, nor for their great practicality, nor because they are fashionable and of the moment, but heed Edmond's wisdom – be sure you will love it until you die. If you are buying for someone else, eccentric, appropriate, amusing, useful and relevant are all words you should add a question mark to. If any or all of those words apply, then buy.

Finding inspiration

Antiques have a gentleness not common in our age, and there is often great beauty in the most ordinary of old objects. You may find yourself inspired – and inspire others – to start unusual and fascinating collections. Sellers often specialize in one particular type of item, and have the knack of arranging their wares in an enticing display. The keys photographed here could inspire a whole wall display at little cost. Bowls and baskets of old balls of string are not only useful but beautiful as well. After getting over the initial shock of receiving a bundle of vintage buttons, I feel sure that, on a dreary winter's afternoon, even a sullen teenager might be moved by the subtle beauty of the buttons and sew them onto an old jacket. They would offer a touch of originality that, in this age of mass marketing, is increasingly difficult to come by.

ABOVE: *An eclectic selection of antique finds.*

BELOW LEFT: *Keys cleverly displayed can make a work of art.*

BELOW: *Button cards are always useful when renovating clothes.*

Paintings and picture frames

You will often find old paintings for sale, many of them by keen amateurs and some of them very fine. It takes time to trawl through the stands but it could prove an extremely rewarding exercise – everybody has room for one more painting and should you be clever enough to find one whose subject is relevant to the recipient, all the better. If you can't find a suitable painting, look at the multitude of frames for sale and paint or make your own picture.

Antique books

Old, leather-bound books are intriguing and the more random the subject, the better. I am usually initially drawn to beautiful binding, and the contents are secondary. However, old books on, for example, country walks or even midwifery can not only be informative but often hilarious – how to skin and cook a rabbit might well be handy if predictions for our future turn out to be accurate! Gardening books never lose their practicality, and are often filled with good advice long forgotten since pesticides and noxious chemicals took the place of tried-and-tested natural remedies and fertilizers.

China

Saucers that long ago parted company with their cups make lovely soap dishes or (dare I say it) ashtrays. A mish-mash of unmatched cups looks divine hanging on a dresser. Decorated plates are perfectly acceptable if they are not of a matching set, and could form the start of a collection. Jugs – small, large, plain, patterned – are lovely planted at Christmas time with a single hyacinth bulb, or snowdrops about to burst into flower. One of these wrapped with gauze makes a fine gift, as does a beautiful cup and saucer filled with home-made, or bought, confections or bath preparations.

ABOVE: *A cup and saucer, filled with confectionary or dried flowers, make a fine gift.*

BELOW LEFT: *A mish-mash of paintings, always worth looking through.*

BELOW: *Books add warmth to a room and wisdom to a brain.*

Presents for men

Men, whom I find particularly difficult to buy for, are perhaps easier to cater for at antiques fairs. For example, it might perhaps be regarded as an insult to give a gift of a walking stick bought from a department store to any man of any age. However, an old, beautifully carved, well-loved walking stick is always a pleasure to take out on a walk. If you give a man a plastic measuring tape, I can't help but feel he might be a little disappointed. Yet one of those hand-crafted leather and brass tape measures could become a treasured possession, even though he may never use it for the purpose for which it was originally intended.

The following list gives some ideas for antique gifts for the most challenging people to buy gifts for – men and teenagers – along with their less inspiring present-day alternatives.

Antique gift ideas for men

▶ Leather and brass measuring tape (present-day alternative: plastic and steel measuring tape)

▶ Old leather collar boxes (present-day alternative: a set of plastic storage boxes)

▶ Hand-carved walking stick (present-day alternative: a lightweight aluminium crutch)

▶ A perfect second-hand tweed hacking jacket (present-day alternative: a designer jacket – an unlikely gift)

▶ An old wicker picnic basket (present-day alternative: a new wicker picnic basket – why buy new when there are so many already made?)

▶ Silver flask (present-day alternative: ditto)

▶ Books (present-day alternative: any books of any age are always a delicious gift)

▶ Painting (present-day alternative: anything of any merit is certainly way beyond my budget)

▶ Beautifully crafted garden tools (present-day alternative: I would be happy with anything to do with the garden but old tools have a pleasing feel)

▶ Old glass cloches (present-day alternative: new glass or plastic cloches)

▶ Clocks (present-day alternative: not so pleasing)

▶ Pocket watch (present-day alternative: there isn't one)

▶ Armchair (present-day alternative: a strange gift)

▶ Desk light (present-day alternative: a sad gift)

▶ Glass decanter (present-day alternative: shiny, lumpy and new – not quite the same)

▶ A set of old terracotta pots (present-day alternative: shiny and new and frost proof – I wouldn't be pleased)

▶ Enamel compost bucket or two (present-day alternative: a pair of plastic buckets)

▶ A collection of beautiful, wooden-handled corkscrews (present-day alternative: a metal corkscrew)

▶ A lovely bundle of antique silver forks tied with string (present-day alternative: a posh canteen of silver cutlery)

▶ A collection of different types of string presented in an old wooden bowl (present-day alternative: a ball of string)

Antique gift ideas for teenagers

▶ An old cocktail glass or two (present-day alternative: a set of pint glasses – not good to encourage heavy drinking)

▶ An interesting painting relevant in some way to the recipient (present-day alternative: a poster)

▶ A hand-made, pure white, lace-trimmed, floor-length Victorian nightdress (present-day alternative: pyjamas)

▶ An old-fashioned (in good condition) board game – encourages social interaction (present-day alternative: play station – encourages a solitary life)

▶ A beautiful old compass in a leather pouch (present-day alternative: an A–Z)

▶ A beautifully leather-bound book – relevant in some way to the recipient (present-day alternative: a book – unlikely that they will be thrilled with either)

FAR LEFT: *Balls of string make a rather novel arrangement, and nobody can have too much string!*

BELOW LEFT: *A walking stick makes a surprisingly handsome gift for men of all ages.*

BELOW: *Silver cutlery can be bought at antiques fairs for a fraction of the price of new.*

making candles

There's no need to throw away partially burned candles, or to leave them to gather dust in the belief that they somehow look ornamental. It's easy to make new candles, beautiful enough to give away as gifts, by combining the remnants in a decorative container, even re-using an original one.

you will need

Several partially burned candles
Old pan or dish
Decorative container
Sturdy, smooth string
Long pencil
Scissors

1 Heat the candle remnants in an old pan or dish, either by placing it in a microwave for 1–2 minutes, or in a double saucepan on top of the stove. Be very careful not to burn yourself, either on the pan or with the resulting hot wax. The candles can be heated separately or together, depending on their colours and how many there are.

2 When all the wax is melted, remove any wicks that may remain and pour the wax into your chosen receptacle.

3 Cut a length of sturdy smooth string and tie one end to a pencil, which should be longer than the circumference of the container. Make several knots in the other end of the string to weight it down.

4 Push the knotted end of the string into the wax with the pencil, and then lay the pencil across the receptacle. Move to a cool place to set.

5 When the wax has set hard, cut the string, leaving enough exposed to make a wick.

Caring for antiques

There are a few do's and don'ts for keeping antique items looking as beautiful – or perhaps even more so – as when you bought them.

Antique textiles

Old textiles are extraordinary. The fact that something as simple as a plain linen sheet, woven by hand on a loom and stitched together to cover a mattress, may still be changing hands today for a great deal of money is worthy of contemplation.

Cotton and linen

Luckily, cotton and linen are robust and sturdy fabrics, and respond well to washing. Most cotton and linen pieces can be gently hand washed, or washed in the machine on a gentle cycle. Never use hot water to wash delicate items. You must also never use chlorine bleach on antique fabrics. Lemon juice will do just as good a job, but remember to rinse the fabric in warm water as soon as you have dissolved the stain. Consult the many remedies for stained fabrics that can be washed in Chapter 1.

Silk and embroidered fabrics

Intricately embroidered pieces or fine silks might need expert advice before cleaning. Try to avoid dry cleaning – unless expressly advised – as the chemicals used may well do more harm than good. Steaming is a good and gentle alternative, although it is still worth taking advice before proceeding.

Storing textiles

Never store textiles in dry, hot attics, nor damp cellars. Ideally, the temperature should be kept constant and humidity at around 55 per cent.

Antique clothes

Do not store antique clothes on a hanger; instead, lie them flat. If possible, roll rather than fold them as the fabric weakens along the folds. If a large item, such as a quilt, has to be folded, lay acid-free tissue paper along the line of the fold to prevent deep creasing. Once or twice a year, re-fold the item to prevent permanent lines forming.

Preventing textiles from fading

Keep precious textiles, including framed needlework, vintage cushions, antique quilts

BELOW: *Old French linen is becoming more and more rare, and thus more and more expensive.*

and rugs, out of strong sunlight. If you have a large and precious rug that, of necessity, has to be left left in strong light, turn the rug regularly so that the natural fading will be equal on both sides.

Drying in sunlight

The sun will bleach robust white fabrics beautifully. Do not dry delicate items in the sun because this will contribute to their demise. Never dry precious coloured washable items in the sun, as they will fade. Sometimes this is desirable: there is many a time I have transformed a garishly coloured item into a beautiful, faded antique with the help of the sun and some lemon juice.

Drying delicate items

Never hang delicate items to dry; always lay them flat on a cotton towel. Otherwise the weight of the water combined with gravity could well rip the fabric, especially if it is lace.

Machine washing lace

If you have a fairly robust item decorated with fine lace, place it in a net bag or pillowcase before putting in the washing machine and washing on a gentle cycle.

Rug and carpet care

Keep precious rugs clean with regular vacuuming. If you feel they need washing, find an expert rug cleaner. If you are having difficulty finding one, ask your supplier who will undoubtedly know of a reputable cleaner.

Many rugs woven in Afghanistan, India or Africa are most probably much more robust than you might imagine. In order to give their handicraft a more lived-in, aged patina, makers often lay carpets in the road for cars to drive over – they come to little harm and just get more beautiful. Remember this when you find yourself delicately dabbing at a stain.

Silver

Browsing in antiques markets can often yield great silver purchases. Complete sets of silver cutlery are usually more expensive than when sold loose, so consider buying single pieces.

Hand washing

Be very careful when washing metal pieces that have a baize or felt covering on the base, such as silver candlesticks and wine coasters. Do not immerse in water. Wash upside down or wipe with a damp cloth.

Wax drippings

To remove wax drippings from an intricate candlestick, turn it upside down and, holding it over a piece of old newspaper, blow hot air from a hairdryer to melt the wax. Don't throw away the newspaper. Instead, fold into a long strip lengthways and tie into a knot to make an excellent firelighter.

Wooden handles

If you are cleaning items with wooden handles, such as silver teapots or coffee pots, polish the handle with beeswax before cleaning the silver part. This will protect the wood from damage by water.

Dusting silver

Keep silver dusted with a soft paint brush. If you dust with a cloth, you are more likely to scratch the surface.

Storing silver

When storing silver, keep a large piece of chalk in the drawer to prevent tarnishing.

Washing in a dishwasher

You can wash silver cutlery in the dishwasher but never with other metals such as aluminium or stainless steel. If you do, the silver will tarnish unnecessarily.

rosebud pot pourri

Scented herbs and flowers, often complemented by a variety of spices, have been used since Roman times to perfume rooms, repel insects, such as ants, and ward off germs. Nowadays, pot pourri is often used ornamentally, displayed in a variety of decorative dishes and containers. Any herbs, flower buds or petals can be used, but sometimes it's nice to concentrate on just one flower, such as these pretty rosebuds.

you will need

Rosebuds
Newspaper
Orange
Lemon or lime
Vegetable peeler
China bowl
Cinnamon sticks, cardamom pods
or whole nutmegs (optional)

1 Collect as many rosebuds as you can through the spring and summer and spread them out on newspaper or in trays to dry, preferably in the sun.

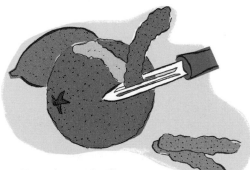

2 Pare the peel off an orange and a lemon or lime. Cut into strips and lay them out to dry with the rosebuds.

3 Meanwhile, find a china bowl that you would like to display – buy one from an antiques fair or second-hand shop if necessary. When the rosebuds and the peel are completely dry, mix them all together in the bowl with your hands. If you want a spicier aroma, add some cinnamon sticks or cardamom pods, or whole nutmegs.

covering a book with vintage fabric

Many treasures are to be found in second-hand bookshops or on the bookstalls of antiques fairs. An old book on a relevant subject makes a thoughtful and unusual present. Covering it in a scrap of vintage fabric makes it unique.

you will need
Vintage fabric
Scissors
Hardback book
Fabric glue

1 Cut out the fabric to the size of the book plus an extra 2.5cm (1in) all round. Open the book, lay it face down and cover the outside with fabric glue. Turn it over and position it carefully on the fabric, allowing the 2.5cm (1in) border all round.

2 If the book has a wide spine, cut the fabric on each side up to the spine, top and bottom. Cut off the resulting flap of fabric, leaving a small amount to tuck in down the spine.

3 Fold in the fabric at each corner, then fold in the edges and glue them down.

4 Glue the first page onto the cover to hide the glued edges.

Glass

Antique glassware is often especially beautiful but its fragility demands special care.

Washing

When washing fine antique glasses, never put them into the sink together. Line the basin with a tea towel to make a padded base. Fill with lukewarm water and add a cupful of vinegar. Wash them one at a time very carefully – old glass is often finer then modern glass and will easily chip or crack. Do not use very hot water because this can crack fine glass.

Drying

Air dry glass by placing it upside down on a flat surface on a clean, dry tea towel.

Cloudy glass

If you have problems with cloudy glass – also known as 'sick' glass – try soaking it in vinegar. Sometimes, however, this bloom found in old glass is permanent. If the item is particularly precious to you, you could seek the advice of an expert.

Decanters

See page 30 for hints on cleaning the hard-to-reach insides of glass decanters.

CAUTION
Never put old, fine glass in the dishwasher – it is always best washed by hand.

Wood

There is real joy in looking after old wood to bring out its natural beauty.

Waxing wood

Never over-wax wooden objects. A thin layer of beeswax three or four times a year is ample. Polish off the wax with a soft cloth following the grain of the wood. Building up many fine layers of wax is the way to achieve a deep patina. Too much wax is difficult to remove and attracts dust.

Dusting ornate wood

Keep wooden objects free from dust, using a soft brush to remove dust on intricate carved pieces, including picture frames.

LEFT: *Antique glass decanters in good condition are often more beautiful than new versions.*

Paper
Storing prints and documents
Handle old prints and documents with great care, if you need to handle them at all. To store, separate them with sheets of acid-free tissue paper.

Dusting books
Keep old books free of dust as much as possible using a soft brush especially for this purpose. With the book closed, flick the dust away from the binding. Always remove books from their shelves before dusting.

Precious prints
When framing precious prints, make sure that the framer inserts acid-free backing paper to preserve the print. If you buy a framed print of particular importance, it is worth taking it to a framer to insert acid-free paper even if the frame seems perfect.

Display prints
Strong sunlight damages and fades paper and artwork. If possible, display framed prints out of sunlight.

Remove staples
Always remove staples from paper – if left in, they will cause rust marks.

Ceramics
Washing
To wash items, use a small amount of detergent or white distilled vinegar in lukewarm water.

Mended china
Never submerge mended pieces of china in water because this will weaken the glue.

RIGHT AND FAR RIGHT: *A random collection of china on a market stall. Try to buy pieces that are uncracked if they are to be used for serving food or drink.*

Drying
As with glass, always dry items by lying them carefully on a folded tea towel.

Removing stains
To remove stains from within a china or ceramic cup, soak with a solution of white distilled vinegar, adding some bicarbonate of soda for difficult stains.

Dusting ornate pieces
For dusting intricate pieces, use a medium soft watercolour paint brush to get into the little crevices.

Finally ...

If you have read this book from cover to cover, I hope it will have made an impact on the way you live – day to day. If ecological issues become so much part of all our lives, we will begin to take for granted that light switches are never left burning unnecessarily, that we never throw things away that can be recycled or re-used, that we never leave water running unnecessarily.

If we refuse to accept plastic bags and excessive packaging, then without noticing we will be making a huge difference. If, as a matter of course, we order bulky non-perishable items via the internet once every three months, then our shopping can be done in an old-fashioned, wholesome way – on foot with a shopping basket. If we are buying produce seasonally, with as few intermediaries as possible between source and purchase, we can have an idea of how our food is produced.

If we just stop, take stock of the way we live and do 12 of the things listed below every day for the rest of our lives, then we will make a difference. If we can delay global warming for long enough to work out a plan to reverse it, then we can, together, feel less ashamed when we hand our beautiful planet over to the next generation.

▶ Switch off all unnecessary lights
▶ Switch off all appliances with a standby light
▶ Shower for one minute less every day
▶ Use grey water to water the garden and wash the car
▶ Boil only enough water to fill your immediate needs
▶ Grow three herbs
▶ Grow ten flowers
▶ Walk instead of using the car once a week
▶ Take at least one of your holidays at home during the year
▶ Plant grass instead of installing decking
▶ Recycle all your paper
▶ Only use recycled lavatory paper

- Try using the cleaning products listed in this book for one whole month
- Make sure every present you give this year has been enjoyed by someone before
- Buy a water filter and only buy bottled water in extreme emergency
- Place a litre bottle filled with water or a brick in your lavatory cistern
- When you buy your next car, make it as environmentally efficient as you can bear
- Ask shops why they are heating the pavement
- Ask shops why they keep their lights on through the night
- Ask shops if it is necessary to have automatically opening doors which are activated by people walking by and not by people walking in
- Choose ten products per week made or grown by organic methods
- Read labels – not for a product's calorific content, but for its green credentials
- Read labels and try where you can to buy produce made in your own country
- Buy local
- Buy seasonal
- Cook from scratch using what you have grown
- Store what you have grown
- Switch your computer and printer off when you stop using it
- Print only those things that are absolutely necessary
- Turn your heating down, and wear more clothes
- Buy an ordinary old-fashioned hand-held fan so for an hour or two a day you can switch off the air conditioning
- Take the train instead of an aeroplane
- Take a bicycle instead of the car
- Walk to your destination once a week
- Teach your children to respect the planet
- Learn to respect the planet

useful contacts

Energy

www.clearviewstoves.com
Manufacturer of clean wood and multi-fuel burning stoves.

www.dunsterwoodfuels.co.uk
Suppliers of biomass boilers and accumulator tanks for storing large volumes of cheap hot water.

www.electrisave.co.uk
Providers of devices to put over your electricity meter, allowing you to work out how much energy is being used by individual devices.

www.energy-crops.com
A co-operative of wood-pellet fuel producers who provide a local supply of high-quality fuel.

www.genersys.com
Information on supplying up to 70 per cent of your hot water requirements in an environmentally friendly way.

www.genvex.co.uk
Heat-recovery ventilation and air-source heat pumps.

www.good-energy.co.uk
Renewable sources of electricity.

www.greenfuels.co.uk
Bio energy consultancy.

www.nef.org.uk
The National Energy Foundation, giving advice on reducing carbon emissions through using energy-efficiency measures and renewable energy sources.

www.solartwin.com
A reliable and easy-to-install solar panel water-heating system.

Food

www.abel-cole.co.uk
A long-established organic food delivery service.

www.agoldshop.com
An old-fashioned grocery shop selling traditional foods, situated at Spitalfields in the east end of London.

www.boroughmarket.org.uk
A beautiful covered market, open on Fridays and Saturdays in the heart of London. Make sure you visit Turnips, a stall selling produce from a collective of farmers and growers.

www.enjoyfrance.com/directory
Farmers' markets in France.

www.farmaround.co.uk
Supplying food from small organic farms in the UK and co-operative farms in Sicily, France and Spain. None of the food is airfreighted.

www.farmersmarkets.net
Farmers' markets in the UK.

www.foodupfront.org
Check the website for local food suppliers.

www.nealsyarddairy.co.uk
A magnificent emporium of cheeses, dairy produce and freshly baked bread.

www.riverford.co.uk
Organic vegetable delivery service.

www.aqualogic-wc.com
Supplier of WaterGreen syphon pump, for
syphoning bathwater into the garden.

Home
www.cabbagesandroses.com
For natural cleaning products, beautifully
packaged and fully sustainable; antiques and
vintage items and hand-printed vintage linens;
clothing and fabrics.

www.dutchtub.com
Lightweight hot tubs which do not require
a pump or electricity.

www.eco-age.com
Fulfils all ecologically sound needs in the home.

www.greenshop.co.uk
Sustainable, eco-friendly products for the home.

www.wwf.org.uk
Information on the campaign to reduce the use
of toxic chemicals.

General
www.ecovy.com
Star- and dove-shaped biodegradable plastic
balloons.

www.futurefriendly.co.uk
Website giving ideas on creating a more planet-
friendly lifestyle.

www.mooncup.co.uk
Cleaner, more hygienic alternative to tampons.

Farms and Gardens
www.dalefootcomposts.co.uk
Suppliers of bracken-based compost.

www.greenfix.co.uk
Specialists in installing rooftop gardens.

www.soilassociation.org
An independent non-profit body that sets organic
standards, supports and advises organic farmers
and works to change the way the UK farms.

index

pests
    gardening, 96, 108–12
    household, 25, 42–5
petal sugar, 129
pets, 43, 147
pewter, 24
phosphorus, 106
picture frames, 173
plant pots, newspaper, 86
plants see gardening
plastic, recycling, 38
plastic bags, 37
polish, beeswax, 20, 32,
    181
ponds, 102
pot pourri, rosebud, 179
potatoes
    peeling, 26
    storage, 125
poultry manure, 76–7
presents, 132, 169–75
preserves, 132–42
preserving pans, 134
prints, care of, 182
propagating, 82–93
puppies, accidents, 43

Q
quince jelly, 139

R
rabbits, 113
rags, 20
rainfall, 60, 100, 102
raspberries, 128
    raspberry and herb
        cordial, 140
    raspberry leaves, 157
rats, 42
recycling
    antiques, 169–82
    clothes, 49
    in the kitchen, 37–8
redcurrant jelly, 138
refreshing morning bath
    tonic, 162
refrigerators, 26, 30, 32,
    62, 120
relish, apple, 142
rhubarb, 110

ring marks on furniture,
    26
rodent pests, 42
root vegetables, storage,
    125
rosemary, 157
    bath teas, 162
    dark hair care, 165
roses, 90
    rosebud pot pourri, 179
    rose petal sugar, 129
rotation of crops, 111
rugs, care of, 178
Russian comfrey, 158
rust
    on cooking utensils, 30
    stains, 27

S
safety
    herbal remedies, 147
    kitchen hygiene, 33–6
sage, 158
    lotion for sunburned
        skin, 160
St John's wort, 153–4
    lotion, 160
salads, rinsing, 26
salt, body scrub, 162
Saracens root, 158
scalp care, 165
scrubbing brushes, 20
seasonal food, 119
seasonal guide, gardening,
    94–9
seed compost, 84
seedlings, netting, 110
seeds, 82–90, 113
sell-by dates, 36
setting point, jam-
    making, 135
shampoo, dry, 165
sheets, 56
shoes, 52
shopping
    herbal remedies, 147
    local produce, 36, 37,
        118–19
shower curtains, mildew,
    30

showerheads, limescale,
    26
shrubs, encouraging
    wildlife, 112
silk, antique textiles, 177
silver, care of, 30, 178
silver fish, 25
sinks, waste disposal
    units, 27
sinuses, blocked, 160
skincare, 166
    age spots, 167
    body scrub, 162
    cucumber lotion, 161
    exfoliation, 167
    oatmeal bath bags, 162,
        163
    sage lotion for
        sunburned skin, 160
sloe gin, 141
slugs, 108–10
smells, removing, 24
snails, 108–10
soda, 20
soft fruits, storage, 128
soil
    compost, 72–7
    crop rotation, 111
    fertilizers, 105–7
solar power, 67
Solomon's seal, 154
sore throats, 160
spices, 149
splinters, removing, 167
sprains, Epsom salts for,
    167
spray bottles, 20
stain removal
    carpets, 24, 32
    on clothes, 53
    cups and teapots, 30,
        182
    deodorant stains, 24
    fruit stains, 25
    on mattresses, 30
    rust stains, 27
    wine stains, 26
stale odours, 27
staples, in paper, 182
steam inhalation, 160

steam irons, 27
sterilizing jam jars, 134
sticklewort, 148
stinging nettles, 156
stings, bee, 160
storage
    antique textiles, 177
    clothes, 49–50
    larders, 120–1
    paper, 182
    preserves, 132
    silver, 178
    vegetables, 122–5
store cupboard
    ingredients, 120–1
strainers, jelly, 134
strawberries, 119
    strawberry face pack,
        166
    strawberry jam, 136
sugar
    jam-making, 135
    petal sugar, 129
sulphur, 106
sun
    bleaching textiles,
        178
    fading textiles, 177–8
sunburn
    cucumber lotion, 161
    sage lotion for, 160
supermarkets, 36, 37,
    117, 118–19
sweet violet, 158
sweet woodruff, 154
sweetcorn, storage, 125

T
talcum powder, dry
    shampoo, 165
taps, limescale, 26
tea towels, 33
teapots, stains, 30
teas
    bath teas, 162
    herb teas, 149
teenagers, gift ideas, 175
textiles
    antique textiles, 177
    covering books, 180

author's acknowledgements

Thank you to my publishers Cico Books, especially Cindy Richards who had enough confidence in me to ask me to write this book, and Gillian Haslam and Marion Paull for their help in editing. To Lucinda Symons and her assistant Francesca Day who spent many days making beautiful photographs, and to Christine Wood for making it all coherent and even more beautiful.

To Chris and Lucy Rich for their exquisite farm and shop providing inspiration for all, and Emmeline Johnston for allowing us to photograph her perfect allotment. To all at Cabbages & Roses, especially Linda Cardona, Amy Gibbons and Kate Strutt, and to my family Mark and Edward Strutt for letting me write in the kitchen. To John and Jack Robinson for cabbages and blackcurrant juice.

And to all those who are making us aware of our beautiful, beautiful planet and are working towards solutions to save it.